So What?

So What?

The definitive guide to the only business questions that matter

Kevin Duncan

Contains over 250 utterly crucial questions

CAPSTONE
be inspired!

John Wiley & Sons, Ltd

Other Wiley Editorial Offices

John Wiley and Sons Inc., 111 River Street, Hoboken, NJ 07030, USA

Jossey-Bass, 989 Market Street, San Francisco, CA 94103-1741, USA

Wiley-VCH Verlag GmbH, Boschstr. 12, D-69469 Weinheim, Germany

John Wiley and Sons Australia Ltd, 42 McDougall Street, Milton, Queensland 4064, Australia

John Wiley and Sons (Asia) Pte Ltd, 2 Clementi Loop #02-01, Jin Xing Distripark, Singapore 129809

John Wiley & Sons Canada Ltd, 6045 Freemont Blvd, Mississauga, ONT, L5R 4J3, Canada

Wiley also publishes its books in a variety of electronic formats. Some content that appears in print may not be available in electronic books.

Anniversary Logo Design: Richard J. Pacifico

Library of Congress Cataloging-in-Publication Data

Duncan, Kevin, 1961-
  So what? : the definitive guide to the only business questions that matter / Kevin Duncan.
    p. cm.
  "First published in 2007 by Capstone Publishing Ltd. (a Wiley Company) … Chichester, … UK"–T.p. verso.
  "Contains over 250 utterly crucial questions."
  Includes index.
  ISBN 978-1-84112-793-4
  1. Communication in organizations. 2. Questioning. 3. Problem solving. 4. Assertiveness (Psychology) 5. Business enterprises–Decision making. I. Title. II. Title: Business questions that matter.
  HD30.3.D86 2007
  658.4–dc22   2007034342

Typeset in 12/16 pt ITC Garamond by Thomson Digital
Printed and Bound in Great Britain by TJ International Ltd, Padtow, Cornwall, UK

This book is printed on acid-free paper responsibly manufactured from sustainable forestry in which at least two trees are planted for each one used for paper production.

Substantial discounts on bulk quantities of Capstone Books are available to corporations, professional associations and other organizations. For details telephone John Wiley & Sons on (+44) 1243-770441, fax (+44) 1243 770571 or email corporatedevelopment@wiley.co.uk

"Charm is a way of getting the answer yes without asking a clear question."

Albert Camus

This book is dedicated to the special people in my life: my inspirational mother Anne; my absolutely brilliant daughters Rosanna and Shaunagh; and my supremely tolerant partner Sarah Taylor.

In memory of my father James Grant Duncan, 1923–1989.
"The best philosopher I have ever met."

ACKNOWLEDGEMENTS

I love chatting about businesses. A big shout goes out to all my mates who run them and listen to my incoherent ramblings: Simon Docherty, Mark Earls, Tina Fegent, John Hamilton-Hunt, Dave Hart, Rassami Hok Ljungberg, Cathy Johnson, Daf Jones, Mark Joy, Graeme Leno, Nic Ljungberg, Jim Marshall, Melanie Ryder, Paul Speers, Glyn Taylor; all the gang at Turner Duckworth, especially Moira and Bruce; and the great team at Prontaprint Victoria.

For taking the time to read and comment on the first draft: Rita Clifton, Jo Cooper, Mark Earls, Mark Giffin and Don Williams. I appreciate it.

A big thanks too to my new team at Capstone, particularly to John Moseley for believing in my stuff. And finally many thanks to the good people at *The Week* magazine ("All you need to know about everything that matters") – the source of the majority of the quotations in this book.

ABOUT THE AUTHOR

Kevin Duncan worked in advertising and direct marketing for twenty years. For the last eight years he has worked on his own as a business adviser, marketing expert and author. He teaches at Canterbury University, and advises various businesses as a non-executive director, business strategist and trainer.

He has two daughters, Rosanna and Shaunagh, and lives in Westminster. In his spare time he travels to strange parts of the world, releases rock albums and flies birds of prey.

Also by Kevin Duncan:
Teach Yourself Running Your Own Business
Teach Yourself Growing Your Business

If you would like to be told of new titles by the author, or want to contact him:
kevinduncan@expertadvice.co.uk
expertadviceonline.com
kevinduncan.typepad.com

CONTENTS

Introduction: Understanding the Value of Questions

Children do it instinctively. They constantly question everything. *So what? Why? Yes, but why? Are we there yet?* They are impatient, and they want to learn. But as we grow older, we lose our inquisitiveness. And we lose quite a lot of our energy. Until, in many cases, we don't actually know why we are doing what we are doing. We just roll along with the same old routine, accepting the status quo without question. This has become a recurring theme in the training sessions that I run. Everyone is apparently overworked, but when confronted with simple, direct questions about *why* they are so busy, they do not have any sensible answers that your average person in the pub would understand.

Let's look at it another way. A person should, within reason, only do what they want to do. And yet many people do all sorts of things, particularly at work, without knowing *why* they do them. This is partly because they do not ask in the first place why something needs to be done. Often, nor does the boss. How scary is that? Have you ever considered that your boss may not even have asked why something needs to be done? And thus begins an unholy chain of vagueness that no one seems prepared to challenge. It's a bit like forgetting someone's name. You get one chance at the beginning and that's it. Once a task is requested, no one seems to have the balls to go back and question it.

So this book is all about the questions that can make a real difference. They work particularly well in business, but can also help hugely in your personal life.

If everybody in business responded with a question when asked to do something, then all the irrelevant stuff would immediately be weeded out. Imagine having 80% of your time freed up every week because you don't have to do the stuff that doesn't get you, or the company, anywhere! Read on.

I keep six honest serving-men
(They taught me all I knew);
Their names are What and Why and When
And How and Where and Who.

From The Elephant's Child by Rudyard Kipling

So What?

This chapter covers how to use the So what? *cycle of questions, and explains the difference between using them internally (privately asking yourself) and externally (asking other people). Inquisition is something of a lost art, and there is much we can learn from children about how to do it well. It is important to get your feelings out into the open, organize them, and interlock them with those of others. There is also a knack to working out what not to say, and when not to say it.*

How to use the *So what?* cycle of questions

I have subtitled this book "The definitive guide to the only business questions that matter". This description may sound a bit over the top, but my orientation is one of simplicity, not complication. There is no intellectual high ground being taken here – quite the opposite. What I am suggesting is that if, as grown-ups, we could recapture some of the inquisitive nature that we had as children, then we would be a great deal more successful, and very much happier.

The question *So what?* is the beginning, or the end, of a series of questions that children instinctively ask, and which we often now fail to ask. *So what?* provides the initial screen: what's the point of this then? If a good reason is provided, then we want to know *Why?* in some detail. Assuming the idea or project passes that test, then we are on to asking *How?*, *Who?*, *When?*, *Where?*, and so on. You may think that all these questions are naturally covered in modern business, but I can assure you that they are not. Once all these elements have been thought through in a satisfactory way, there are a number of sense-check questions to make sure that we haven't overlooked something. These are *Do we really need to do this?*, *Something must be wrong if...* (a sentence you have to complete), and *Are we there yet?* The *What?* question is left as a postscript at the end because, frankly, if you haven't worked out what you are doing in the first place, then you shouldn't be embarking on the other questions at all.

Which brings us back to the beginning. The diagram in Figure 1.1 shows the cycle, but don't worry, we'll work our way through the whole thing during the course of the book.

THE SO WHAT? CYCLE OF QUESTIONS

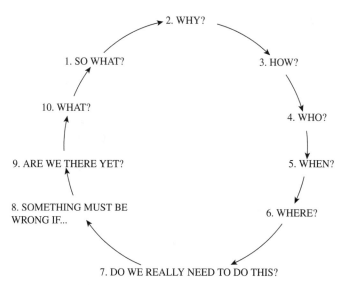

Fig. 1.1: The *So What?* cycle of questions

How to use the *So what?* question

So what? is a very powerful question in its own right. It can deflate the most cerebral and lofty minds in one stroke. Somebody makes an assertion and does not expect to be challenged. But they certainly *should* be challenged. You don't have to be massively confrontational, but you do need to make your own point and stand your ground. So let's investigate the tone in which the *So what?* question should be delivered. It can certainly be used with devastating effect by sarcastic teenagers, as a derogatory measure – the "Am I bovvered?" syndrome. But that is not the style I am suggesting here. *So what?* has use both as an internal question and an external one. In other words, you can ask it of yourself as well as others. Let's have a look at the difference.

For internal use only?

It is perfectly possible to use all the questions in this book to sort your thoughts out without ever having to say them out loud. If you are self-employed, or a decision-maker in a company and do not wish to reveal your thought processes to your colleagues, then you can ask all the questions in this book *of yourself.* The questions are just as valid, and a very useful way of sense-checking your thinking.

> "Only he who handles his ideas lightly is master of his ideas, and only he who is master of his ideas is not enslaved by them."
>
> **Lin Yutang**

Internal *So what?* questions

So what? questions are essentially infinite, and the reader will instinctively know which issues to address, but first here are some examples of internal ones.

- I hate my job: so what?
- I feel out of my depth: so what?
- I have been told to do it: so what?
- I am in charge: so what?
- I am very busy: so what?
- I have a grand title: so what?
- I disagree with a colleague: so what?

Your first step is to pose a lot of questions. Don't shirk the tough ones because, if you address them honestly, they will help you the most. The next step is to work out what your answers to the questions are, and what you propose to do as a result. For example:

State of affairs	Answer: what I am going to do about it
I hate my job: so what?	(a) Change something (b) Leave this job and get another one
I feel out of my depth: so what?	(a) Get help (b) Enjoy the challenge and learn more
I have been told to do it: so what?	(a) Do it and stop moaning (b) Ask my boss for a reason
I am in charge: so what?	(a) Enjoy the moment (b) Redefine what I do each day
I am very busy: so what?	(a) Keep going and hope I can take it (b) Think harder about which bits matter

I have a grand title: so what?	(a) Use it to enforce helpful ideas
	(b) Get rid of it and be more humble
I disagree with a colleague	(a) Don't mention it
	(b) Say so and propose an alternative

My purpose here, and the purpose of the questions, is not to be an irritant but to flush out the potential answers that are really going to help you. If there are no questions, or they are too vague and general, they will not help you at all. Rubbish in, rubbish out, as the saying goes. So think hard and get to the heart of the matter early.

> *"What you have to remember is that civil servants use vagueness and ambiguity with razor-sharp precision."*
>
> **Anonymous senior civil servant**

External *So what?* questions

External *So what?* questions are equally infinite. They can go on and on. The knack with them is never to ask just one, but to know when to stop when the issue is becoming sufficiently clear. Here are some examples:

- That's your opinion: so what?
- This is my opinion: so what?
- You are my boss: so what?
- I don't have a clear opinion: so what?
- I disagree with all my colleagues: so what?
- The company line is announced: so what?

State of affairs	Answer: what I am going to do about it
That's your opinion	(a) I agree, so we're okay (b) I don't agree and I'm going to say so
This is my opinion	(a) You agree with me, so we're okay (b) You disagree, so we need to discuss it
You are my boss	(a) I'll do whatever you say (b) You pay for my opinion, so I am going to give it to you
I don't have a clear opinion	(a) I am happy to roll with whatever is suggested (b) I need to think and develop one
I disagree with all my colleagues	(a) I need to persuade a number of them (b) I am incompatible with the company and need to find another job
The company line is announced	(a) I agree, so all is well (b) I disagree, so I need to say so

Now try a few of your own. Try filling in the panel:

State of affairs	Answer: what I am going to do about it
_____	_____
_____	_____
_____	_____
_____	_____

The art of inquisition

The Spanish Inquisition gave the word a bad name, but inquisition is a thoroughly desirable thing. Without it, everybody rushes around doing things without really knowing why. In a previous book, I introduced the idea that you should never do anything unless you know why you are doing it (*Teach Yourself Running Your Own Business*, p. 91). It sounds so obvious, and yet every time I ask people in my training courses why certain items are on their list of things to do, the answers are less than convincing. Think about it. Never do anything unless you know why you are doing it.

Inquisition: the act of inquiring deeply or searchingly; a deep or searching inquiry

---

Put simply, if more people were more inquisitive more of the time, we would start a chain reaction of good things. Let's imagine:

- Your boss is more inquisitive, so he or she is less likely to ask you to do pointless things.
- You are more inquisitive, so you are less likely to accept instructions to do pointless things without asking why.
- Your boss knows you are inquisitive, so he or she thinks even more carefully before suggesting something pointless.
- You get less stupid stuff to do, so you enjoy your job more.
- Everybody gets the hang of it, and the whole company starts concentrating on the important stuff instead of the trivia.
- Profits go up.
- Your pay goes up.

Another way of looking at this relationship is to view it as a pair of linked equations.

The Inquisition Equations

1. *Demanding, thoughtless boss + passive, meek employee = status quo*
2. *Demanding, thoughtless boss + inquisitive employee = change of ingrained habitual behaviour*

In the first scenario, nothing changes. The boss gets away with slack thinking, and the subordinate does nothing about it, leading to an unsatisfactory working relationship. In the second scenario, the boss has to react, and suddenly the employee is in the driving seat. Power to the people! And just before you cry out that you never contradict your boss, bear in mind that one of the biggest complaints that bosses have is that their staff never come up with any ideas.

> *"A timid question will always receive a confident answer."*
>
> **Charles Darling**

There's the rub. Asking timid questions will only ever lead to two things:

1. You fail to make your point.
2. The other person enjoys a second opportunity to ram home theirs.

Weak questions are no help to you at all. They make you look daft, neuter your capability, and ultimately lead to you not enjoying your work. So don't ask them.

Learning from children

Children are the experts at inquisition, albeit often in an annoying manner. Their persistent lines of inquiry frequently leave us exasperated. You know the sort of thing.

Child: Why is that man fat?
Parent: Because he has eaten a lot.
Child: Why has he eaten a lot?
Parent: Because he was hungry.
Child: Why was he hungry?
Parent: Because he hadn't eaten for a while.
Child: Why hadn't he eaten for a while?
Parent: Look, he just hadn't, all right?

This is hardly a satisfactory explanation for a young inquiring mind, and as a grown-up, you certainly shouldn't be fobbed off with half-baked answers and poorly thought-through requests. Don't stand for it. Tell them what you feel.

Venting your feelings

Venting your feelings is no bad thing. Most of us these days get paid for our opinion anyway, and we have every right to express them. Equally, as a consequence of doing so, we must be prepared to defend them and expect a robust response from someone who does not hold our view.

> *"Every man has the right to utter what he thinks truth, and every other man has the right to knock him down for it. Martyrdom is the test."*
>
> **Dr. Johnson**

The trouble with feelings, of course, is that, annoyingly, other people have them too. So we are not just grappling with yours, but everybody else's. And in business, that person could well be your boss or a customer. It is much easier to blurt out a fact than a feeling that you may not be able to substantiate, and yet, in many contexts, it is the feelings that resonate more powerfully and may hold the power to generating better ideas. Indeed, in many businesses these days, they call it passion, and value it very highly. On the continent, they have been doing this for centuries.

In essence, control represents containment (holding things back), and feelings offer a springboard for imagination (unleashing potential). This balance of yin and yang is at the very heart of any decent business.

Sticking it to the man

Most bosses aren't half as good as they think they are, nor as good as they would like you to believe. In their private moments, they all think they are still in short trousers anyway. Many are simply getting away with it. It is your job to stand up to them. Give them a run for their money! Are you a man or a mouse? Are *they*? It's time to "stick it to the man", as the rock vernacular goes.

> *"Keep your head down and always wear brown."*
>
> **Father's career advice to his son**

This appalling piece of advice was given to a friend of mine by his father. I think we'll keep that one anonymous, don't you? This is not how it works in the modern world. Work out what you stand for, and let them know, in a charming and engaging way, of course.

The power of feelings

> *"There is no opinion however absurd, which men will not readily embrace as soon as they can be brought to the conviction that it is generally adopted."*
>
> **Schopenhauer**

Feelings can be highly persuasive. It rather depends on how they are presented. The facts will speak for themselves to a large degree. So will the control factors – the constraints that apply to the business issue, such as production capability, budget, resources, time limits, and so forth. But it takes personality to bring an opinion to the fore and argue its case. The question is: are you just expressing your own bias? If so, is that of any benefit to the matter in hand?

> *"Everyone is a reactionary about subjects he understands."*
>
> **Robert Conquest**

Twittering on about your small sphere of interest or your long-held prejudices is unlikely to create the right conditions for the big idea or a clever solution, so consider whether your perspective is simply too narrow to be of use in this particular context. If it is, bow out of the discussion or get informed quickly so that you can contribute in a helpful way.

The importance of getting feelings out in the open

Of course, you could argue that the less you know, the more useful you can be in many contexts, and this may well be true if pure objectivity is required. How often have you heard it said that someone is "too close" to the subject to have a sensible view?

> *"Not to expose your true feelings to an adult seems to be instinctive from the age of seven or eight onwards."*
>
> **George Orwell**

It seems that in many cultures, both national and corporate, there is something of a conspiracy or hidden rule that prevents people from being allowed to air their views without fear of recrimination. Don't open your mouth in case your boss frowns upon it! Say nothing until you are spoken to! Unfortunately, this approach is useless in business.

> *"If you're working on things that everyone accepts, you're not working on anything."*
>
> **Alan Snyder, American scientist**

So it is perfectly healthy and natural to be sitting in a room violently disagreeing with someone, or several people. Ask *So what?* regularly. Remember, you were probably hired for your opinion so you can hardly be criticized for expressing it, and it is certainly preferable to sitting around violently *agreeing* with each other. There will be plenty of time for that later, when you actually know what you are doing, and in what direction the solution to the matter in hand is heading.

> *"Think for yourself, and let others enjoy the privilege of doing so too."*
>
> **Voltaire**

So we want your thoughts out on the table, and that means allowing others to do the same thing too. You can't have it all your own way! The knack is to organize your thinking so that it is clear to you, clear to everyone else, and helpful to the debate. Keep asking *So what?*

> *"A problem shared is a problem halved, so is your problem really yours or just half of someone else's?"*
>
> **David Brent, The Office**

Directional and pointed lines of inquiry

Feelings and opinions are essential in providing direction to creative thinking, particularly in business, precisely because they are directional and pointed. When they are clearly articulated, it is often called leadership. You know the sort of thing:

Boss: *"I have a dream and it's somewhere over that hill!"*
Staff: *"We like that dream, so we'll go over that hill!"*

They have no more idea as to what is over the hill than the boss does, but because they like the direction, they will gladly follow. Charismatic leaders have the power to inspire.

Feelings are pointed. They cannot always be explained, but they are often inspirational in creative thinking.

> *"Whatever you may be sure of, be sure of this: that you are dreadfully like other people."*
>
> **James Russell Lowell**

Organizing your feelings

Organized feelings: an oxymoron or a helpful idea? Many would argue that this is a contradictory notion. Surely, feelings just *are*? And don't they spill out whether you like it or not? Mmm. Not necessarily. With a little thought it is quite a simple matter to work out what your feelings are, jot them down, arrange them, edit them, and work out which ones help the subject in hand, and which ones don't. Once you have got the hang of it, you can apply exactly the same process to everybody else's feelings, so long as they are being honest, and so is the person noting them down.

> *"Nothing is easier than self-deceit. For what each man wishes, that he also believes to be true."*
>
> **Demosthenes**

As the proponent of a feeling, you need to be quite grown-up about it too. Blurting out comments randomly might make you feel better in the very short term, but it usually causes havoc. Just take a couple of seconds to work out your point of view before it comes flying out of your mouth.

> *"'Point of view' is that quintessentially human solution to information overload, an intuitive process of reducing things to an essential relevant and manageable minimum. In a world of hyperabundant content, point of view will become the scarcest of resources."*
>
> **Paul Saffo**

Also bear in mind that sometimes you have to hear yourself say something before you can actually work out whether you believe it or not. The classic case of this is during interviews.

When you are caught on the hop by a question that you haven't thought about, you will always provide some kind of answer. Sometimes it's not until later that day that you can decide whether you believe what you said or not.

> *"The man who sees both sides of the question is a man who sees absolutely nothing at all."*
>
> **Oscar Wilde**

So you need to believe your feelings completely. This helps the other person hugely too, because you can't make any progress if you keep contradicting yourself. Thought is also required if you have multiple feelings on a subject, or there are multiple subjects.

Who cares about other people's feelings?

> *"It is as absurd to argue men, as to torture them, into believing."*
>
> **John Henry Newman**

You can't force someone into believing something, nor can you blame them for having a strong point of view, otherwise you would be a hypocrite, because you presumably have one yourself. So don't try to steamroller them with your views, and don't do down their opinions. Regard the whole thing as an interesting exchange of views. Listen hard and work out the common ground.

> *"There is no such thing as conversation. There are intersecting monologues, that is all."*
>
> **Rebecca West**

Interlocking your feelings with theirs

Interlock your feelings with those of your colleagues. Only by doing this will you make any progress. Most forward motion in business is halted by stubborn behaviour and entrenched opinion. This can be resolved in a few minutes with a bit of mature thought and a clear mind. Self-employed people make quicker decisions and get things done more quickly because they sort things out in their own heads and get on with it. Corporations take twenty times longer to do this because people can't agree and don't work hard enough to air and sort out differences efficiently and rapidly (see "Corporate time moves slower than normal time", *Teach Yourself Running Your Own Business*, p. 78).

> *"The trouble with having an open mind, of course, is that people will insist on coming along and trying to put things in it."*
>
> **Terry Pratchett**

Taking your opinions and stubbornly restating them is no route forward. Intelligent people can entertain another person's view without necessarily agreeing with it. It is also worth remembering that there is essentially no right and wrong in business, just an opinion that ultimately prevails. So keep an open mind, and change it if you are confronted with a better idea.

> *"Minds are like parachutes; they work best when open."*
>
> **Thomas Dewar**

The interlocking of two sets of feelings can be viewed and expressed in many other sets of ways. It could be two different companies with different opinions on a proposed deal. It could be the customer in relation to the company. It could be male and female contrasting views. What it essentially boils down to is the distinction between what's in it for you, and what's in it for me.

> *"Imagining what it is like to be someone other than yourself is at the core of our humanity. It is the essence of compassion, and the beginning of morality."*
>
> **Ian McEwan**

To crystallize your thoughts, answer each of these questions in one short sentence, and write it down.

- What do I feel about this issue?
- If there are multiple issues, repeat the process for each one.
- Is there anything else?
- What does the other person feel about this issue?
- Is there anything else?

Now reduce the issues down to as few as possible. Summarize each feeling in one word if possible.

What not to say, and when not to say it

> *"For a marriage to have any chance, every day at least six things should go unsaid."*
>
> **Jill Craigie**

Do also bear in mind, that some things are better left unsaid. This does not mean that you should negate your own feelings. Clearly, if it matters that much to you, then it must be said. But be diplomatic, rather than strident. A strong view is a strong view. It doesn't need to be blared through a megaphone at point blank range to have the desired effect. However, some feelings are simply antagonistic without contributing anything of merit. Here are some examples.

Pointless expressions of feelings

"That's utter crap."
"I hate it."
"You always say that."

Helpful, directional expressions of feelings

"I don't like it at all, but I can think of a better idea."
"I don't think that idea A works, but idea B certainly could if modified a bit."
"If we just concentrated on X, would you be satisfied?"

> *"Probe with a bayonet: if you meet steel, stop. If you meet mush, then push."*
>
> **Lenin**

Intelligent lines of inquiry reveal flaws in flabby thinking, and it is your job to find the weak points. The purpose is not to humiliate your colleague or assert your intellectual authority, but simply to work out if something is essentially nonsense. There is too much of it about, frankly. So what we are after here is the expression of feelings that offer direction. I call it pointy thinking.

The power of pointy thinking

There is no point in having a massive dust up and blurting out all sorts of feelings if no alternative direction is offered up in the process. Imagine several people doing that. There would be scores of opinions flying around, with no helpful resolution on the table for consideration. A hopeless state of affairs, in all probability leaving a trail of bruised egos and an important business issue unresolved. Does that remind you of any business meeting you have been in, I wonder?

> *"When elephants fight, it is the grass that suffers."*
>
> **African proverb**

Pointy thinking aims to clarify all of this chaos. The enemies here are vagueness and hurtful expression of pure emotion. They simply don't help at all. You need to marshal your feelings, work out whether you truly believe them, and express them in simple, clear terms so that the other person can work out what your point is.

> *"How can 65,000 people do anything other than agree on something unspecified on an unspecified date?"*
>
> **Zac Goldsmith on the Earth Summit**

It may not have escaped your notice that the opposite of pointy thinking would be point*less* thinking. It is also your job to make sure that you are not being so vague as to be unintelligible to the other person, nor simply digging in for the sake of it.

> *"It is difficult to get a man to understand an argument when his salary depends upon his not understanding it."*
>
> **Upton Sinclair**

Getting the mix right

Progress is only ever defined by consensus. You only need a little bit of agreement to move forward. Don't try to agree on everything, and don't try to fix everything at once. Just pay attention to the other person's opinion, and look hard for areas of common ground. Don't keep repeating your position – look harder at theirs to achieve progress.

> *"The essence of liberty is not that my interests should be tolerated, but that I should tolerate yours."*
>
> **Tom Stoppard**

Conceding ground to make progress

This is particularly important if your point of view is partial or only recently formed. How strong is it? How much do you really believe in it? If, privately, you can see holes in your own argument, then don't press the point. Try saying nothing, or saying that you don't know. Then everyone can move on.

> *"Learn to say 'I don't know'. If used when appropriate, it will be used often."*
>
> **Donald Rumsfeld**

Equally, don't give in on something just because someone else is shouting louder than everyone else, being a bully, or pulling rank. None of these actions make their opinion any more valid. There will be moments when you have to stick to your guns, and you should, so long as you have thought your feelings through comprehensively.

> *"You can always spot a well-informed man – his views are the same as yours."*
>
> **Ilka Chase**

Stay strong on your opinion, even if your boss is vehemently disagreeing. There is no merit in simply reflecting their views because of their position. They will respect you much more if you restate your view calmly and clearly, and, so long as you are not just being stubborn for the sake of it, you will make progress together. No one likes a lily-livered individual.

> *"He had a whim of iron."*
>
> **Anthony Powell on John Betjeman**

The difference between an instruction and a true purpose

Just because you are ordered to do something does not mean that it serves a purpose. Don't tolerate it. Of course, the army relies on blind acceptance of orders, otherwise the battlefield would be a random bunch of people wandering about doing what they fancied. But, despite all the macho literature telling you that it is, business is not war. It should be a robust exchange of opinion leading to a decent outcome, and serving a commercial purpose. Never forget it. Many a gung-ho leader has used the language of war to describe business activities – campaigns, tactics, strategy, blitzes, assaults, attacks, and of course the hideous "targeting", which has now been turned into a highly unsatisfactory verb. Don't fall into the trap of using this lazy and pseudo-macho language. I guarantee that it will simply increase the likelihood that you are talking poorly thought-through nonsense.

Summary of *So what?* thinking

> *"You have to know how to accept rejection, and reject acceptance."*
>
> **Ray Bradbury**

In essence, *So what?* thinking boils down to a few simple principles:

1. Acknowledge that feelings are just as relevant as facts and control factors.
2. Get them out in the open.
3. View them as directional and pointed.
4. Organize your feelings – this is not a contradiction in terms.
5. Be honest about them, and say that you don't know if they are too thin or unformulated.
6. Pay attention to other people's feelings.
7. Interlock them with yours and find areas of common ground.
8. Stick to your guns if you fervently believe in something.
9. Concede ground if necessary to make progress.
10. Use the consensus to launch your initiative.

So what? summary

- Consider how to use the *So what?* questions carefully.
- Work out whether they are for internal use only.

- Draw up your lists of internal and external *So what?* questions.
- Embrace the art of inquisition.
- Learn from the approach of children.
- Vent your feelings using directional and pointed lines of inquiry.
- Think about what *not* to say, and when not to say it.
- Express your feelings in a helpful, directional way.
- Consider the power of pointy thinking.
- Concede ground to make progress.
- Spot the difference between an order and a true purpose.

> *"It is better to have a known enemy than a forced ally."*
>
> **Napoleon**

However, on the assumption that there is some basis for agreement, we can now get to grips with the *Why?* question.

Exercise: Expressing your feelings

1. Write down your own feelings on the topic in question. One is ideal, two is okay, and three is the maximum. Any more than that, and we won't be able to make sense of the resulting mess.

2. Start each feeling with "I believe..." Write each one down and read it back to yourself. If, on re-reading, you are less sure about it, then re-phrase it or throw it in the bin. Remember, no more than three.

3. Either get the other person to do exactly the same exercise from their perspective or, if you are quite clear what they think, write their opinions down facing the other way. Take the time to make sure, however, that you are not distorting or misrepresenting their views.

4. This shows you how to overlap the two sets of feelings. Some opinions may overlap, some may not. Exclude irrelevant feelings that neither of you can agree on. If at all possible, try to sum up each feeling in one word to make sorting them out easier.

5. Check the areas of overlap. In most cases, assuming reasonable people and common goals, there should be some. If there is not, then have an earnest conversation until you can find some. If, eventually, you conclude that there are none, then nothing can help you reach agreement. You will simply have to fall back on one of two old rules:

   (a) The boss's opinion wins.
   (b) The one nearest the mantelpiece wins (Monty Python, 1979).

Why?

This chapter covers what the question Why? *can mean. For what reason? For what purpose? For what cause? It introduces the* Why? *chromosome and shows how being inquisitive leads to success and job satisfaction. Writing a list of what you are not going to do can be as helpful as what you are going to do. Constructive questioning can reveal better ideas than those you currently have. Taking the edge off the* Why? *question and using constructive questioning can lead to powerful results.*

The power of *Why?*

Why? is arguably the most powerful word in the human language. Any fool can come up with an idea. Anyone can suggest a hypothesis, or a reason. Anyone can assert a supposed fact. But their claims and statements must be able to withstand the scrutiny of the all-powerful *Why?* question. *Why?* is a superb debunker. And a great deflator. It punctures pomposity and reveals bullshit in a split second. That's why those prone to waffling, and people who duck questions, absolutely hate it. You'll rarely hear an evasive person answer it. Politicians almost never do. It's just too raw and too honest. Which is precisely why it is so brilliant. Deployed for your own purposes, it is a razor-sharp blade that can clear your mind and fix your purpose. Asked of others, it can reveal the truth and generate true direction. In both cases, it could massively improve your quality of life, assuming you are prepared to spend the necessary time actually thinking, rather than fizzing around like a fly in a bottle, expending energy on all the wrong things.

> *"Many people would sooner die than think. In fact they do."*
>
> **Bertrand Russell**

One of the reasons that people dislike the question so much is that, assuming they actually answer honestly, it forces them to think clearly. This in return will probably reveal that they have not thought particularly clearly until that very moment. If this is exposed in front of other people, the embarrassment can be complete, precisely because it is revealed in the presence of the very people whom you would least like to observe it. So it is best used as an internal question first, so that you are not on the receiving end of such embarrassment (see Chapter 1, For internal use only?). And if you choose to use it on someone else, be aware of its awesome power (see How to use the *Why?* question).

What *Why?* means

Why: for what reason, purpose or cause?

Well, you can't get much clearer than that, can you? How many times have you embarked on something without considering:

1. The reason?
2. The purpose?
3. The cause?

I guarantee that, even if you stop reading this book now, you will improve your life if you consider these three points carefully from now on. The *Why?* question has the ability to filter out hundreds of pointless activities, clarify thousands of decisions, and generate vast amounts of additional time for you to do the things that you really *do* want to do. Rather than dwelling on trivia that has no bearing on the important stuff, or twaddle that your boss has generated to keep you occupied.

Why? For what reason?

Everything needs a reason, and everyone needs a reason. Human nature demands it. But this is not a pure philosophy book (although it is hugely interested in how people choose to view the world), so we will move swiftly on to the basic reasons why reason plays such a big part in how you conduct your life and your working behaviour.

> *"It's all right to have a train of thoughts, if you have a terminal."*
>
> **Richard R. Bowker**

Thoughts have to arrive somewhere, or else they just fly around in the ether and serve no purpose. In the same way, an idea remains useless until it is enacted. Having a train of thought(s) is fine, but keep it to yourself until you know where you have arrived. We have all worked with people who insist on thinking out loud. It is a deeply irritating characteristic of vague people, and there is now a whole industry based around it. Consider this approximate chain of events:

1. I am responsible for a particular project.
2. I am not clear-minded enough to sort it out myself.
3. I fail to think the problem through properly.
4. I offload my incoherent ramblings onto a colleague.
5. Nothing happens.
6. I call a brainstorm.

Ring any bells in your company? This sort of nonsense goes on all the time in business, and it's got to stop.

Blurting out unformulated rubbish in the corridor doesn't work. It is demeaning and hugely unproductive. Convening a bunch of disinterested colleagues with irrelevant skills in a nasty room with tepid tea and cheap sandwiches doesn't either. If you want a sensible answer, ask yourself *Why?* first. If you cannot solve it yourself, ask it calmly of one expert colleague, whilst simultaneously passing on your own lines of inquiry so that they don't go down the same blind alleys. Or turn your *Why?* question into a stimulating one-line brief for someone who might be able to solve it.

> *"Understanding the reasons for an avalanche does not, I suppose, make one any the more grateful for being pinned beneath it."*
>
> **Alistair Maclean**

Bear in mind that the answers you get might not be that palatable. No one said the results would be pleasing. But they should be accurate and informative to the extent that you can conclude what you think of a certain state of affairs, and be able to work out what to do next. Also, consider that the reasons themselves are not responsible for the action that needs to be taken as a result of their presence. It's the business equivalent of don't shoot the messenger, and it is your job to unearth the truth and push on to the most appropriate conclusion.

> *"No snowflake in an avalanche ever feels responsible."*
>
> **Stanislaw Jerzy Lec**

Now, let's move on to look at reason in a modern business context.

> *"All that is beautiful and noble is the result of reason and calculation."*
>
> **Charles Baudelaire**

There is a school of thought that suggests that the presence of reason on its own is not enough to prevail in the topsy-turvy world of modern business. The idea is half right. I am not advocating a slavish adherence to pure reasoning or logic, nor a linear dependence on process. Quite the opposite, in fact. I just want you to know the reason why you are doing something every time you do it. That really shouldn't be too hard to establish if you adopt the right lines of inquiry.

> *"Reason is no match for power and prejudice, armed with force and cunning."*
>
> **William Hazlitt**

I have put this quotation in as a counterpoint. I don't want to believe it, but if you are completely overwhelmed in your company by politics and conniving so-and-sos, then I suppose it might be right. If that really is the case, then I recommend that you find another job. After asking yourself *Why?*, of course.

Why? For what purpose?

The reason for something is one thing. Its purpose is equally important. If you have no purpose to your actions, then what's the point? (That last question could easily have been a chapter in its own right.) A purpose is a truly wonderful thing. Take a look at the range of its definitions.

Purpose:
1. The reason for which anything is done, created, or exists.
2. A fixed design, outcome, or idea that is the object of an action or other effort.
3. Fixed intention in doing something; determination.
4. Practical advantage or use.
5. That which is relevant or under consideration.

Any or all of these can provide wonderful focus. Every time you do something, or are asked to do something, you should establish for what purpose. Take a second to ponder on how much you do in your working life that has no purpose. How much time do you spend travelling, in meetings, and generally doing stuff that has no bearing on the main purpose? If the amount is a large percentage of your working day, week, month or year, then I suggest you pause to reconsider immediately and make some changes.

> *"It is better to debate a question without settling it, than settle a question without debating it."*
>
> **Joseph Joubert**

At this stage in the inquisition, we are not rocketing towards an immediate solution. We are simply trying to establish why things are as they are, and what might usefully be done about it, if at all. We are still in the business of exposing issues and woolly thinking that previous, more vague, lines of inquiry have not uncovered.

Ultimately, though, you will certainly want your efforts to have an effect, and that means working out the straight-line relationship between what you do and what might happen as a result. (For a full rundown on the basic principles of cause and effect in business, have a look at Action and chain reaction, *Teach Yourself Growing Your Business*, p. 154).

Mark Earls, in his excellent book *Welcome To The Creative Age*, pushes this even further by introducing the notion of purpose-ideas. In other words, what matters about an idea is its purpose, and what really counts is what you want to change about the world. A big idea for the individual perhaps, but the principle holds true – don't do anything unless you have worked out what you are trying to achieve. For a quick summary of the thinking in his book, have a look at the Appendix.

Why? For what cause?

You have to have a cause, otherwise you'll always be wondering why you are doing anything, and coming up either with no answers, or unsatisfactory ones.

Cause:
1. A person, thing, or action that produces an effect.
2. Grounds for action; motive; justification.

If a person produces no effect in their work circumstances, then what are they doing there? We return to a recurring theme of this book – that you are paid for your opinion and need to express it regularly. And when you do, you will be wanting to have an effect on something or someone.

Whydunnit?

You will all have heard of the film and book genre, the Whodunnit? Fewer people may have come across the Whydunnit? This is a novel or film concerned with the motives of the criminal rather than his or her identity. This drives to the very heart of the *Why?* question. We know that a crime has been committed. Clearly someone was responsible. But the inquiring mind may well be more interested in the *Why?* than the *Who?* (See Chapter 4 for a full rundown on the *Who?* angle.)

Why are we here?

Stripped down to basics, the *Why?* question lies at the essence of any sentient being. One of the differentiating aspects of the human race is that, as far as we know, we are the only creatures to question our very existence. Why are we here? Rhetorical perhaps. Unanswerable probably. But crucial to the livelihood of any inquiring mind, and the wellbeing of any business worth its salt that is trying to move forward.

> *"Thinking is the very essence of, and the most difficult thing to do, in business and in life. Empire builders spend hour-after-hour on mental work... while others party. If you're not consciously aware of putting forth the effort to exert self-guided integrated thinking... then you're giving in to laziness and no longer control your life."*
>
> **David Kekich**

The notion of control is a tricky one. I personally would never assert that you can completely control your life. But you can have a damn good go at having a huge bearing on what you do, so that, *more often than not*, you are doing the things that you want.

How to use the *Why?* question

The *Why?* question has to be handled carefully. It is too powerful and poignant to be blurted out in a confrontational way without considering the consequences. Why? Because it can come across as abrupt and shocking to those who are not ready for it. If you know the person well, you might be all right. If the person is touchy, or your boss, or you are in mixed company, you might want to lace the pill a bit. But let's start first with internal *Why?* questions, which may be hard to take, but which cannot cause offence because you are asking them of yourself specifically to get to a better answer.

Internal *Why?* questions

As with *So what?* questions, *Why?* questions are potentially never-ending. You will know instinctively what needs to be addressed, but here are some ideas. To start with I have deliberately dealt with exactly the same ones as in the previous chapter, so you can see how different questions applied to the same issue lead you in very different directions.

- I hate my job: why?
- I feel out of my depth: why?
- I have been told to do it: why?
- I am in charge: why?
- I am very busy: why?
- I have a grand title: why?
- I disagree with a colleague: why?

Now, let's look at how the *Why?* question pushes you into areas that *So what?* did not.

State of affairs	Answer: possible reason
I hate my job: why?	(a) It is boring (b) I don't like the people
I feel out of my depth: why?	(a) I don't have the skills (b) I have been over-promoted
I have been told to do it: why?	(a) They don't know why either (b) For political or power reasons
I am in charge: why?	(a) I am the best person for the job (b) There was no one else and I got lucky
I am very busy: why?	(a) I am thoroughly disorganized (b) There is genuinely too much for me to do
I have a grand title: why?	(a) I asked for it (b) Everyone round here has them
I disagree with a colleague: why?	(a) They don't get it (b) I don't get it

I am not suggesting for one second that these are the real reasons why. They are merely examples to give a flavour of what might be the case, and wherever possible I have chosen extremes to highlight the fact that you may actually be in the wrong. That's the beauty of internal *Why?* questions – you can ask them of yourself and sort out your point of view before going public and making a fool of yourself.

External *Why?* questions

External *So what?* questions are equally infinite. They can go on and on. The knack with them is never to ask just one, but to know when to stop when the issue is becoming sufficiently clear. Here are some examples:

- That's your opinion: why?
- This is my opinion: why?
- You are my boss: why?
- I don't have a clear opinion: why?
- I disagree with all my colleagues: why?
- The company line is announced: why?

State of affairs	Answer: possible reason
That's your opinion	(a) You know what you are talking about (b) You are toeing the party line
This is my opinion	(a) I know what I am talking about (b) I am blindly copying everyone else
You are my boss	(a) You are better than me at the job (b) You are a brown-noser and got lucky
I don't have a clear opinion	(a) It doesn't bother me that much (b) I haven't thought about it enough
I disagree with all my colleagues	(a) They are all right and I am wrong (b) I am right and they are all wrong
The company line is announced	(a) It is a genuine step forward (b) It's the same rubbish repackaged

Now try a few of your own. Try filling in the panel:

State of affairs	Answer: possible reason
_____	_____
_____	_____
_____	_____
_____	_____

"Three pipe" problems

So you can see how the *Why?* question creates a more open-ended set of answers. They are not definitive solutions in their own right. They frequently lead to other questions, which is completely fine so long as you don't leave the *Why?* questions hanging and fail to attend to them. You must pursue the line of inquiry to its complete conclusion. If it's a big, hairy issue, then give it the time and attention it deserves. Sherlock Holmes always used to smoke a pipe when mulling over a murder inquiry. Tricky ones might require enough time to smoke two pipes. And particularly difficult inquisitions he would describe as a "Three pipe problem". So spend the time, and learn to identify which issues are easy to attend to, and which are three pipe problems.

When asking *Why?,* stick to the facts

No one ever got fired for sticking to the facts. Amazingly though, although it sounds almost incredible, many business discussions take place *in the absence* of the facts, thereby rendering them practically useless. Equally, many ideas are generated that refuse to acknowledge the facts, and as such they end up being unusable.

Contrary to the popular jargon, try thinking *inside* the box. Just stick to the facts first. In some cases, this can be a very fast process, depending on the complexity of the task. It is also essential to have present the people who actually know the facts, not those who are skimming, or pretending that they do.

As a small diversion, do you know the origin of the phrase *think outside the box?* Everybody uses it these days (see my aversion to jargon in Chapter 4), but few people know where it comes from, which is poor. You should not feel comfortable bandying words and phrases around when you don't really know what they mean. It comes from the Gottschaldt figurine, or nine-dot game. There are three rows of three dots, forming what looks like a nine-dot box or square. The challenge is to join all the dots without taking your pen off the paper, using no more than four straight lines. The point is that, if you think of the dots as a box, you can't solve it.

The precise origin of the nine-dot game is actually the source of some debate. The explanation above comes from Wayne Lotherington's book *Flicking Your Creative Switch*, which includes all sorts of clever ways in which to have more original ideas. However, in *The Art Of Creative Thinking*, John Adair claims to have introduced the idea himself in 1969. He believes that once you understand the creative process, you can train yourself to listen, look and read with a creative attitude. Chance favours the prepared mind. By keeping your eyes open, listening for ideas and keeping a notebook, you can capture stimuli as they occur.

His techniques include:

- Using the stepping stones of analogy (use normal things to suggest new uses).
- Making the strange familiar and the familiar strange (analyse what you don't know about something you know well).
- Widening your span of relevance (many inventions were conceived by those working in other fields).
- Being constantly curious.
- Practising serendipity (the more you think, the more it appears you are in "the right place at the right time").

THE GOTTSCHALDT FIGURINE

Fig. 2.1:   The Gottschaldt figurine

- Making better use of your Depth Mind (trust your subconscious to sort things out and generate solutions once you have "briefed it").
- Learning to tolerate ambiguity.
- Suspending judgement.
- Not waiting for inspiration – you have to make it happen.

Both books are summarized in the Appendix.

> *"Discovery consists of seeing what everyone has seen and thinking what nobody has thought."*
>
> **Anon**

If this brain-teaser is driving you mad, then you can relieve your misery by looking at the Appendix.

The *Why?* chromosome

You have heard of the X- and Y-chromosomes that have such a bearing on our sex and our inherited characteristics.

Well, I would like to introduce the *Why?* chromosome. The idea has two elements:

1. Take the inquisitive nature of childhood and continue it into adult life.
2. Pass it on so that everyone starts asking *Why?* more often.

It's pretty simple, really. Much of what we learn as a child is unlearnt in later life. This is unnecessary and wasteful. Let's be inquisitive grown-ups! And let's start an epidemic of question-asking in companies.

How being inquisitive leads to success and job satisfaction

Without wishing to labour the point, for those of you who doubt whether you have permission to keep posing this question at work, remember this: you are paid for your opinion. Being inquisitive will definitely benefit your career, and will expose the less thoughtful people higher up the chain.

If you need to ask *Why?*, the sooner you do it the better

Boss: *Can you do x?*
Subordinate: *Why?*
Boss: *Errr...*

In this example, the poorly prepared boss has no sensible response, and, frankly, until they do, you need do nothing. If they think of a decent reason later that you are happy to accept, then fair enough. If the request comes in writing, then you are in an even better position.

Boss: *Dave, by copy of this email can you do x?*
Subordinate: *Of course. But first I have a number of questions as to why x will help us. They are a, b, c, …* (the longer this list, the better).
Boss: *! (He never replies.)*

Why bother?

Let's get into a bit more detail about why we want to bother to do anything at all. In the broadest sense, we either do things because we want to (pleasure), or because we need to (work). This is a crass and simplistic definition, but the orientation is about right. So we can push harder towards working out whether something is worth doing at all by asking these types of *Why?* questions:

- Why are we bothering with this at all?
- Why me?
- Why this?
- Why now?

If you can generate satisfactory answers to all of these, you can move on to:

- Why, specifically, is this the proposal?
- Why are we doing it this way?
- Why are we waiting?

And finally, you can press on with the *Why?* questions that allow you to be specific about the other elements you need to know about, which form the basis of the rest of the book. These are:

- Why are we doing it this way? (*How?* Chapter 3)
- Why am I doing it? (*Who?* Chapter 4)
- Why are we waiting? (*When?* Chapter 5)
- Why is this happening here? (*Where?* Chapter 6)

The whole thing then comes full circle when you ask:

- *Do we really need to do this?* (This is a final sense-check of why we are bothering with something at all, recapped in Chapter 7.)

It also hits you straight between the eyes if you try to complete the sentence:

- *Something must be wrong if...* (the subject of Chapter 8).

Write a list of what you are *not* going to do

Once you are completely clear about *why* you are going to do something, it is a pretty simple matter to write down a list of *what* you are going to do. There's nothing earth-shattering about that, until you realize that most people's "To Do" lists are a complete mess. Being as they are, a complete hotchpotch of stuff in no particular order, and usually so long as to be incomprehensible, many lists simply do not do the job for which they were designed. Here is not the place to go into how to write out a decent and effective list. But you might want to try this anti-list idea.

Try writing out a list of what you are *not* going to do. I have a mate who had such a poor experience with one particular employer in his field that he has it written into his career plan never to work for that group of companies again. And, believe me, he could probably double his money if he did. So, what you are *not* going to do is a crucial component of what you *are* going to do. Let's take some examples. Write "*I am not going to...*" at the top of a sheet of paper, and then jot down some of the things that really do not help you be effective.

I am not going to...

- Get involved in Project Watering Can.
- Go into the office every day.
- Travel to Frankfurt every month.
- Attend so many meetings.
- Drink coffee any more.

As you can see, the points can range from the huge to the trivial. Use this anti-list to outline what you won't do, and so clarify the value of what you will do.

Why, oh why? Disgusted of Tunbridge Wells

We've all read the letters pages of newspapers and magazines. Disgusted of Tunbridge Wells writes in to moan about a particular subject, and asks "*Why, oh why, doesn't the government do x about y?*" Very boring, very negative, and usually not very well expressed. Nobody minds someone pointing out that something is wrong or that it doesn't work well (indeed, that is the whole point of *Why?*). But it is essential that this point is combined with a proposed solution. Otherwise you would just be moaning with the rest of them, and that won't get us anywhere. In other words, we can see what the problem is, but what are your better ideas?

Constructive questioning: what are your better ideas?

The *Why?* question forms the basis of constructive questioning – constructive being the operative word. If you are asking the question of yourself, you will want to come up with a better idea to solve your problem. If you are asking it of a colleague, then you must have your own better idea, or preferably several of them, up your sleeve to move the situation on. Otherwise you will just come across as a negative moaner who blocks ideas but never has any good ones of your own.

Taking the edge off the *Why?* question

There will be those reading who find the *Why?* question a bridge too far. Whilst it might be perfectly acceptable to ask it of yourself, in the privacy of your own head, or even out loud to yourself in a quiet room somewhere, it just sounds too raw to ask it directly of someone else. It's a shame really. Why shouldn't we be able to ask *Why?* without causing offence? Here are some possible reasons why the question on its own may not go down well.

- The company culture is rather conservative, and doesn't encourage inquisitive people.
- The company is massively hierarchical, so subordinates are "not supposed" to question their bosses.
- The company is very political, so people only ever suck up to their bosses and never expose their weaknesses openly (although they may well do them down behind their backs).
- Your boss is deficient, and so hates to be questioned.

- Your boss is a bully, and actively punishes questioning behaviour.
- You are very shy, and don't feel you can ask.

We have all come across a lot of companies where these types of issues apply. It doesn't make them helpful or relevant, but they do have to be borne in mind. If the company has a stifling culture, is obsessed with status, or densely populated by political people, then you have three options:

1. Change it, if you have the power.
2. Live with it, if you are too flimsy.
3. Leave, and find something better.

You don't have to be that smart to realize that option number two really isn't one. So change it or leave.

Suppose you do wish to pose the *Why?* question, but without being so naked as to use only that word, and thus run the risk of sounding rude or confrontational. The first option is to use it, but in conjunction with some other words, to take the edge off it a bit. For example:

- Can you tell me precisely why that is?
- Why, would you say, do we need to do it that way?
- In your opinion, why is this so important?
- In comparison with Project Daffodil, why is this higher priority?
- Why has this suddenly become a priority?

You get the idea. Invent your own. Just put a bit of verbiage round the killer word in order to sweeten the pill a bit. I am not a massive advocate of this, but I am trying to aim off for those of you who favour a less confrontational approach. Just promise me one thing: don't waffle so much as to disguise what you really want to find out. Remember, if you ask a multiple question, you won't receive a decent answer. Keep it short, preferably no longer than ten words.

Your second option is to ask why but without using the word. Impossible? Not at all. This chapter is full of ways to get the answer you want without using the word. Have a quick review and see.

- For what reason?
- For what purpose?
- For what cause?
- What is the motive behind this?
- Should we really do this when we could be doing x?
- Don't you think y would be a better solution?

And so on. Don't be duplicitous or mealy-mouthed about it. If you dress it up too much, you won't influence the matter in the way that you want. Just find the right amount of dressing to suit your boss, or the company culture, if you really must. But if you can, just ask *Why?*

Summary of *Why?* thinking

Why? thinking boils down to a few simple points.

1. Question everything, because you can.
2. Understand that being inquisitive is a powerful attribute.
3. Never do anything unless you know why you are doing it.
4. Do not blindly accept an instruction.
5. Ask for the reason.
6. Ask for the purpose.
7. Ask for the cause.
8. Stick to the facts and don't get emotional.

9. Be constructive, and always offer better ideas.
10. If you really must, take the edge off it but still push for the answer you need.

Why? summary

- Acknowledge the power of *Why?*
- Understand what *Why?* means, and use it carefully.
- Whydunnit? Sometimes the motive is more interesting and revealing than the act itself.
- Work out why you are here.
- Identify "Three pipe" problems and allow them the necessary thinking time.
- Use the *Why?* chromosome idea to pass on inquisitive behaviour – it leads to success and job satisfaction.
- Write an anti-list of what you are *not* going to do.

Exercise: Getting constructive questioning right

1. You are furious with your boss, because they have blindly ordered you to do something that will occupy you for a long time (several days or more). This could be something along the lines of:

   (a) Create a long presentation for the Managing Director.
   (b) Conduct an extensive competitive review of the market.
   (c) Draw together a feasibility study.
   (d) Pull together the last five years' figures.

2. If you are lucky, this request will have come by email, thereby giving you time to forge a response. If it was a verbal request, you have lost a little of the initiative by not asking *Why?* immediately, but you can retrieve your position.

3. Write out a list of all the stuff you have been asked to do. Against each request, write down all the *Why?* questions you have. Now choose the appropriate phraseology, medium and timing with which to ask them.

4. Keep an eye on the responses you get, and turn the exercise into a way of life. In all probability, the amount of irrelevant stuff you have to do every day will decrease and you will have a better life.

How?

This chapter covers what How? *means. In what way? In what manner? By what means? Ask* How? *early to avoid disappointment, and make sure that the answer is not vague. Flush out and flesh out how things will be done. Find out how others do it. If you can't answer the* How? *question, you may have to ditch the project. Fire off regular Howitzers to ensure the highest possible chance of moving from concept to reality.*

Time to take stock

Now is the time to pause and take stock of what you have achieved so far. You will have begun your newfound habit of inquisition by asking *So what?* Assuming that you were able to establish a satisfactory answer (or answers), you will have moved on to ask *Why?* Once again, being more inquisitive than the average bear, you will have had to be completely satisfied with the answers that you flushed out. This means that, whatever it is you are about to embark upon, then you must be happy that it is thoroughly worthwhile doing, and that you know precisely why you are doing it. If this is not the case, please heed the warning below.

Warning:

**IF YOU DON'T KNOW *WHY* YOU ARE DOING SOMETHING,
DO NOT READ THIS CHAPTER UNTIL YOU DO.**

There is absolutely no point in working out *how* to do something, if you are not sure *why* you are doing it. If in doubt, ask *Why?* again until you are fully satisfied. It really doesn't matter how many times you go round this loop – never work out the *how* until you have established the *why*. I cannot stress this strongly enough.

The important thing is to reflect calmly on what has been revealed so far. The results need to be examined carefully and objectively, and relieved of any irrelevant material. In most contexts, where there has been disagreement or a difference of opinion, the way forward should now be evident.

The power of *How?*

So let's assume that you are ready to proceed with the implementation of an idea or a project. The power of *How?* is that it has the capability to reveal whether the thing is actually going to get done or not. This sounds simplistic, but it is absolutely fundamental. If an idea doesn't get enacted, then I am afraid it remains just that: an idea. Even more pitiful is when a brilliant idea remains just as a brilliant idea. In fact, there is a school of thought that says that an idea does not technically exist unless it has been brought to fruition. How many times have you stood in the pub with someone who apparently has a brilliant idea?

Bloke in pub: I've got this brilliant idea! *(He explains it.)*
Mate: I agree it's brilliant, but have you actually done it?
Bloke: Well, not entirely…

For a complete rundown on the superb principle of "Things either are or they aren't", look at *Simply Brilliant* by Fergus O'Connell. His point is that the best ideas aren't always complicated and the incredibly straightforward stuff is often overlooked in the search for a complex answer. He suggests seven principles that can be adapted for attacking most everyday problems:

1. Many things are simple – *despite our tendency to complicate them.*
2. You need to know what you're trying to do – *many don't.*
3. There is always a sequence of events – *make the journey in your head.*
4. Things don't get done if people don't do them – *strategic wafflers beware!*
5. Things rarely turn out as expected – *so plan for the unexpected.*
6. Things either are or they aren't – *don't fudge things.*
7. Look at things from others' points of view – *it will help your expectations.*

There is a summary in the Appendix to give you a taster. It's a universal truth. If you haven't done it, it doesn't exist. And if it doesn't exist, then, realistically, it can't be that good, can it? So it is imperative that you work out how to do it, and then get on and do it. Otherwise, see next.

Six months later...

Bloke in pub: I've got this brilliant idea!
Mate: Yes, but have you actually done it?
Bloke: Well, not entirely...

(A groundhog pops his head round the corner and we realize it's all a dream.)

What *How?* means

We have all sat in endless meetings where supposedly intelligent people come up with scores of ideas about what should be done. Somebody writes them all down, types them up, circulates them on email, and stores them in a file. And that's basically where they stay. Unless someone has the ingenuity to work out how they are going to see the light of day. The person who can achieve this is as valuable to the company as the person who dreamt up the original thoughts. As usual, the road to a decent result begins with one of the world's simplest questions: *How?*

How? 1. In what way? 2. In what manner? 3. By what means?

For some reason, *How?* doesn't seem to have the same confrontational effect as *Why?*, but it is no less effective for that, particularly when you examine the nasty issues that have to be dealt with if it is to be answered in a satisfactory way. Let's have a look at what this wonderfully powerful three-letter word really means.

For those of you brought up in Britain in the second half of the seventies, *How* was also a children's television programme in which Fred Dineage and his team explained how all sorts of things worked in the world. Every week they raised their palms and greeted us with the supposedly traditional Red Indian greeting, *How!*

How? In what way?

The way is the route, the method, the technique, or the process. If the company doesn't have it, it may not happen at all. If your boss doesn't have it, he may need you. If you don't have it, where is it coming from? Try these questions to come up with a solution.

- In what way is this going to get done at all?
- In what way is the company going to get this done?
- In what way do you propose doing this?
- In what way do you propose that I do this?

If these questions are an immediate source of embarrassment, then there is something wrong. At one extreme, it might mean that there isn't a cat in hell's chance that it will ever happen. In other words, people never do what they say around here. It may simply mean that you are surrounded by the types of people who love to pontificate about ideas, but who frankly can't be bothered to implement them. Be suspicious of such people. More positively, it may just mean that no one in present company knows how to do it, so a new solution is required. That may mean acquiring the skills, or bringing them in, both of which could be tremendously interesting and enlightening.

How? In what manner?

The way isn't quite the same as the manner. The manner is the style, the fashion, or the *modus operandi*. The project could be fast or slow (see Chapter 5: *When?*). It could be collaborative or dictatorial. It could be done by one person, or by a massive team. It could involve outsourced help, or be completed solely by salaried staff. All the permutations need to be examined to define clearly how the thing will get done. Try answering these questions:

- In what manner is this going to get done?
- In what manner is the company going to get this done?

- In what manner do you propose doing this?
- In what manner do you propose that I do this?

How? By what means?

The means is the resource and the expertise. Any fool can sit in a meeting and initiate a eureka moment. You can hear it now, and you've probably been in just such a meeting: "I've got it! All we have to do is launch product *x* and we'll clean up!" Well done, mate. Absolutely brilliant. Everyone agrees that Nigel is truly inspired for having such ingenuity. Then someone from the back asks: "How exactly are we going to do that then?" Stony silence. The vague rustling of tumbleweed as it drifts metaphorically across the meeting room. Ah. He never thought of that bit, and that's the power of the *How?* question.

So before everyone in the office starts booking their tickets for the Innovation Awards dinner, make sure they ask the *How?* question. Liberal use of it will establish whether the team or the company does have the relevant resources and experience, and help all concerned to avoid early disappointment.

Ask *How?* early to avoid disappointment

How many times have you looked at your checklist and realized that Project Rhubarb has been sitting on it for several months, and nothing much seems to be happening? I don't mean that literally, of course. There is no reason why you would ever have worked on Project Rhubarb. Any project you can think of will do just as well. The point is, projects are always decreed to be the Next Big Thing when they start, but they have a horrible habit of running out of steam, and it often happens really quickly. Sometimes, it happens the next day.

Imagine you are sitting in one of those marvellous meetings: the brainstorm. At the end of it, everybody is really chuffed because there are ten superb ideas on the wall, and Pauline, who was able to pop in for ten minutes at the end after her conference call with New York, has blessed them all. Deep joy. Everyone goes to the pub, leaving the most junior person, Steve, to write up the notes. A quick glance by someone who knows the true capabilities of the team or the company would reveal that most of them won't see the light of day. But no one says anything, because no one wants to admit failure, or contradict Pauline (nickname "Appalling") because she is a power-crazed bitch who tends to fire people who don't "fall into line".

Job prospects aside, this is precisely the time to lob in the *How?* question. It may not be massively popular, but it could save months of fiddling about with unrealistic plans that have little or no chance of ever happening.

"There's no such thing as a bad idea." Yes there is!

Whoever first coined this ridiculous phrase probably reduced the productivity of the Western world by 10% at a stroke. Of course there is! Having a bunch of people sitting around chewing on complimentary sandwiches and all congratulating each other on their marvellous ideas is a complete waste of time. This is political correctness gone mad. Or someone overshot on the idea that the only way to get good thoughts from people is to praise them all the time. This is errant nonsense. A bad idea is a bad idea, simple as that. For bad, read stupid, unrealistic, outlandish to the point of insanity, unoriginal, or any other adjective that denotes that it won't get the business anywhere. It doesn't matter if it came from the tea lady or the Managing Director – it's still rubbish.

In any decent culture, it should be possible to admit this before wasting everybody's time. So, if you possibly can, do not agree to those brainstorms where someone asserts that no idea is a bad idea. They usually add some fatuous postscript along the lines of "we can screen them for viability later", but why not screen them on the spot? That's where the *How?* question comes in.

Working out how: checklist

In what way?	Route, method, technique, process
In what manner?	Style, fashion, *modus operandi*
By what means?	Resource, expertise

How to use the *How?* question

Although *How?* is not quite as in your face as *Why?*, it can still be pretty devastating, as Nigel and the bloke in the pub found out. So let's have a look at some of the ways in which the *How?* question can help you make progress and get things done. Here are some examples.

- We need to get this thing started: how?
- We need to get this thing finished: how?
- My company has promised this project and we have to deliver it: how?
- A boss has promised this project and we have to do it: how?

- I have promised this project and we have to do it: how?
- We do not have the expertise to do this: how (can we get it done)?

Some of these can be asked both internally and externally. Whereas before we have looked at the internal ones first, this time we are going to do it the other way round. This is because the *How?* question frequently involves you or your colleagues taking specific and personal responsibility for something, and if no one wants to, you may have to rethink things yourself to find a way through. For more on this, have a look at Chapter 4: *Who?*

External *How?* questions

All of these questions can be asked in open session. If the responses are unpalatable or unhelpful, then you may wish to retire gracefully and consider them yourself.

State of affairs	Answer: possible way
We need to get this thing started: how?	(a) We have the skills and resources (b) We do not, so we need help
We need to get this thing finished: how?	(a) We have the manpower and we are on time (b) We need more people immediately
My company has promised this project and we have to deliver it: how?	(a) We have the right people (b) We have over-claimed and need outside help
We do not have the expertise to do this: how (can we get it done)?	(a) We fudge it and risk the consequences (b) We get outside help

Establish how *not* to do it

Working out how to do something is hugely helped by establishing how *not* to do it. This has two facets:

1. This is how not to do it.
2. This is how we cannot do it.

They sound the same, but they aren't. The "how not to do it" list will naturally include all the methods that the company has previously used to try to do it, but got it wrong. You can learn from the mistakes of competitors in the same way. In short, therefore, it should become something of a salutary lesson list to make sure all pitfalls are avoided. The second list, "how we cannot do it", is all to do with the capability in the team or the company. If people know what they are doing, then the *How?* could well be easy. If not, it may be insurmountable.

> *"The absence of alternatives clears the mind marvellously."*
>
> **Henry Kissinger**

The point is, the more routes you eliminate, the clearer the way forward will be. Use the checklist to clarify your options.

Project Rhubarb	**How not to do it**
_____	_____
_____	_____
_____	_____
_____	_____

Project Rhubarb	How we cannot do it
_____	_____
_____	_____
_____	_____
_____	_____

Internal *How?* questions

If these lines of inquiry are getting you nowhere, then you might have to work them through on your own. Sometimes, they are directly linked to your workload and expertise. In which case, you may wish to consider:

State of affairs	Answer: possible way
I have promised this project and we have to do it: how?	(a) I pull out all the stops to get it done (b) I swallow my pride and recommend it is cancelled
A boss has promised this project and we have to do it: how?	(a) We do what he says and make it happen (b) We talk him or her out of it

The killer *How?* question

If things remain vague, and frankly they really shouldn't be at this stage, then spend your entire time concentrating on this one expression of *How?*

The killer *How?* question:
How PRECISELY is this going to get done?

This question is so effective that you may well need to ask it many times in a row. Keep going – the results are worth

it. As usual, you may also need to try a few of your own.
Here you go:

State of affairs	Answer: possible reason
_____	_____
_____	_____
_____	_____
_____	_____

No room for vague

There is no room for vagueness when answering the *How?*
question. If someone says, "We'll deal with that later",
then it's a fudge and it probably won't get done. If it's too
detailed an answer, then be suspicious of it. If the language
is circumspect, then it is probably disguising deficiencies
in the solution. If you couldn't describe it to a mate in the
pub, then it's probably too complicated. Complication is the
enemy of *How?* Keep it simple, and stamp out vagueness
immediately.

Indirect *How?* questions: flush out and flesh out

There are, however, some *How?* questions that can be
posed in an indirect way, but they serve a different purpose.
Simple, direct *How?* questions flush out the precise nature
of the route to get something done. Indirect *How?* questions
have the ability to flesh out the subtleties of a complicated
solution. For example:

• Can you give me a flavour of how that is going to
work?

- Can you tell me how that was done before?
- How exactly did you do that?
- How did it happen?
- How did we arrive here?

You can see how these broader questions have the power to reveal some of the more qualitative elements behind a project. The facts of how something can be done have their uses, without doubt, so here we can probe more deeply for the texture, the spirit, and the orientation of the subject matter, in a broader way. Use the direct *How?* questions to flush out the facts, and the indirect ones to flesh out the nuances. Remember, all we are interested in is how we are going to get the job done.

> *"Well done is better than well said."*
>
> **Benjamin Franklin**

Qualitative *How?* questions

The degree to which the qualitative texture of a project or plan is of interest to you will depend on many factors, including how complicated it is, how many people are involved, your level of involvement in it, and your level of interest in the subject matter. But let's assume that this is something that you are very interested in, and scrutinize some of the *How?* questions that you might wish to ask.

How? question	Linked thought
How do I feel about the chances of success?	Do I care if it works or not?
How are we going to benefit from this?	Is it worth doing?

How proud am I of this?	Do I want to be involved or not?
How good is this idea?	Can we do better?
How on earth did we get here?	Have we arrived in the wrong place?
How can we afford it?	Has it been costed properly?

Many of the answers to these wide-ranging questions stray into the murky domain of office procedures, company culture and that old chestnut "how things are done round here". So let's now have the drains up and have a good old look at some dodgy working practices that should have gone out with the ark. Many are still used to stymie great ideas, effectively neutering the *How?* question by simply answering it with "We can't", or "It isn't".

Hopeless answers to *How?* questions

How is this going to get done?	*It isn't*
How can we do this?	*We can't*

This is clearly a pointless and obstructive way to behave, although amazingly it happens in businesses every day. Those who perpetrate these crimes are the killers and jobsworths who delight in saying no but never make anything happen themselves. In any walk of life, these people are a pain in the fundament. Decent-minded people need to unite to expose them.

Jobsworth: a person who invokes the letter of the law in order to avoid any action requiring initiative, cooperation, etc.

We all know who they are at work, but little ever seems to be done about it. Weed them out and get rid of them! Here are some examples to ponder on.

HOW? Resistor Type No. 1: Hackneyed Office Worker

The *Hackneyed Office Worker* insists on following set procedures and as a result cannot think around problems. Process and procedure, that's all this person thinks about. The most creative thing this person has ever done is to choose between beige and dark brown on his second-hand Volvo. Such people will provide hundreds of reasons as to how something cannot be done, whilst offering little in the way of constructive suggestion. Frequently, they simply spend all day blocking every suggestion for forward motion, and strangely always seem to arrive in the pub promptly at 5.30.

> *"Western society is built on overwork during the week and over-consumption at weekends."*
>
> **Dan Kieran**

HOW? Resistor Type No. 2: Horrible Old Ways

The *Horrible Old Ways* exponent refuses to move on and keeps referring to "the good old days". This may be a specific reference to the past, when something was indeed done by a different method. Or it may be a dyed-in-the-wool procedural point such as "We can't do that unless we involve Geoff", or "The company has never done it that way before". To which you would, of course, respond with a robust "*So what?*"

> "*The world is so full of possibilities that dogmatism is simply indecent.*"
>
> **Albert Einstein**

HOW? Resistor Type No. 3: Hunch Overcomes Wisdom

The *Hunch Overcomes Wisdom* sufferer flies in the face of proven experience on the grounds that something "just doesn't feel right". This type of person has no proof, but doesn't like taking risks, and loves to create the impression that he or she has some hard-wired intuition that understands the soul of the company better than anyone else. As well as being massively arrogant, and probably self-deluded, they are also frequently wrong. It is often the case that, shortly after announcing to all and sundry that they are the living embodiment of the company mission statement, they are fired for being "culturally incompatible".

So you should approach the *How?* elements of any challenge with a flexible, open mind, creatively and positively looking for decent ways forward, whilst at the same time deploying a healthy amount of realism so that you or your company aren't charging up pointless blind alleys all the time.

> "*Blessed are the flexible, for they shall not be bent out of shape.*"
>
> **Michael McGriffy**

Simple is good

Equally, struggling for a method that is supposedly unique to your company or truly original could well be a monumental waste of everybody's time. By all means seek originality in your ideas and products, but seek the path of least resistance every time when it comes to the *How?*

> *"I narrow-mindedly outlawed the word 'unique'. Practically every press release contains it. Practically nothing ever is."*
>
> **Fred Hechinger**

The *How?* is often much simpler than we care to admit, and we should celebrate the fact. If the way forward is clear, take it. Do not look for "unique solutions" or "bespoke, tailored channels", just get on and do it with the minimum of fuss. Why would you want the route to getting something done to be complicated? Many businesses deliberately wish to make things complicated, and you would need to be a psychiatrist to explain why comprehensively. Suffice to say that if it takes longer they can charge more, and if it sounds complicated then customers need to rely on them more heavily. The latter, making something deliberately hard to understand, is called obfuscation, and lawyers are past masters at it.

> *"The brain is a wonderful organ. It starts working the moment you get up in the morning and does not stop until you get into the office."*
>
> **Robert Frost**

Subsidiary *How?* lines of inquiry

In the same way that a child asks *Why?* repeatedly until the adult loses the will to live, *How?* can be pursued as a near-endless chain. Don't be afraid to chase it down to the umpteenth level if it really helps you to get to the root of the matter. Start with the basic question and keep pushing. *How? How? How?* If you reach a dead end and are still not satisfied with what confronts you, play with the language a little in and around the core word. Like this:

- How about x?
- How about y?
- How come that is the case?
- How so?
- How's that, exactly?
- However, what about z?

However is an excellent word to help you put an idea on hold whilst not necessarily pursuing it, nor indeed rejecting it.

> *"The mark of an educated mind is to be able to entertain an idea without accepting it."*
>
> **Aristotle**

However means on the other hand, or nevertheless. This enables you to look at other possibilities which might serve your needs better, and help you to answer the *How?* part of the problem more effectively.

How do you do? Finding out how others do it

I am not a great fan of the competitive review, in which you gather all the information you can about the competition in order to see what they are doing. In the extreme, this can lead to the sort of bland benchmarking that has made so many businesses characterless and faceless in recent years. Like all great sports coaches, I would rather ignore the opposition and just decide how you want to perform.

But if you really can't work out how to do something, then as a last resort, you may wish to look elsewhere to see how others do it. This assumes of course that someone somewhere else has indeed worked it out. Bear in mind that, if they have, then your idea may not be that exciting after all – clearly someone else has beaten you to it.

If you can't answer the *How?* question, ditch the project

Eventually, after pursuing every possible avenue, you may have to face the fact that the *How?* question simply cannot be answered. In other words, no matter how good the idea is, it simply cannot be done. To reach this conclusion is not in any way defeatist. In fact, it can be hugely liberating. Thundering on blindly with something when all the evidence suggests that it can't be done is plain stupid. The intelligent person knows when he is beaten. Take it on the chin and do something else.

> *"An idea isn't responsible for the people who believe in it."*
>
> **Don Marquis**

Sometimes the impetus for a project or idea comes from someone, often in a senior position, who has publicly expressed massive enthusiasm for it, and who cannot bear to discover that it cannot be done. Tough. As the quote says, the idea is not responsible, and if it can't be done, it can't be done. At this point, you would be well advised to apply the S.U.M.O. principle in Paul McGee's book. The S.U.M.O. acronym stands for Shut Up, Move On, and in essence he suggests that you accept the facts, stop bleating about it, and move on to the next (more productive) thing. There is a summary in the Appendix.

Firing off regular Howitzers

As with all the questions in this book, it's your job to get into the habit of using them. Although you might solve a short-term problem by asking the *How?* question, it will serve you best if you use it as a way of life. Regularly applied, like a good lotion, it will eradicate pointless activities and dead-end routes that can snarl up your diary for weeks on end. It might help to view the question as a gun that you can aim and fire at any problem whose resolution has not been clarified. Fire off Howitzers regularly, and enjoy the benefits of a clearer diary, and the satisfaction of knowing that you are not pursuing stuff that will never see the light of day.

Summary of *How?* thinking

How? thinking boils down to a few simple points.

1. The power of *How?* is that it sorts out unfeasible ideas from realistic ones.

2. It can be stripped down into three main components:
   - In what way?
   - In what manner?
   - By what means?
3. There is no room for vagueness when answering: it has to be clear and simple.
4. Additional indirect questions help to flush out and flesh out the central method.
5. Finding out how others do it may help to unclog your thinking, but be wary of just copying others.
6. If you can't answer the *How?* question, ditch the project.

How? summary

- Take time to take stock of your position.
- Work out what *How?* means, and ask the question in the right places.
- Consider internal and external *How?* questions.
- Use indirect *How?* questions to flush out and flesh out.
- Keep your eyes open for those who resist *How?* questions:
   - ~ HOW? Resistor Type No. 1: Hackneyed Office Worker
   - ~ HOW? Resistor Type No. 2: Horrible Old Ways
   - ~ HOW? Resistor Type No. 3: Hunch Overcomes Wisdom
- Remember that simple is good.
- Pursue subsidiary *How?* lines of inquiry if they help to add texture to your thinking.
- Fire off regular Howitzers and turn it into a habit.

If you have a eureka moment, you can of course, in the time-honoured fashion of cricket, shout Howzat!

Exercise: Moving from concept to reality

1. Think of a project or idea that needs to come to fruition soon. Write down its essential purpose.

2. Now write the *How?* question underneath. Start to fill in exactly how it is going to get done. If it is complicated, then you will need to ask the question lots of times, and record the answers. Let's say it has ten parts. If you can scribble down fairly quickly how all of them will get done, you are probably onto a winner. If there are huge holes (say, half of them with a question mark against them), then you need to rethink carefully.

3. Review the subsidiary lines of inquiry to see if they provide any new angles. If you can migrate the strike rate to, say, eight out of ten, then you have made good progress, and may be able to resolve the remaining two.

4. Take the remainder and work out how to crack them by thinking outside the norms of what your company normally does.

5. If there are an overwhelming number of unfulfilled question marks that cannot be rectified, you may need to conclude that the project or idea won't work.

Who?

This chapter covers what Who? *means. Which person? Which persons? Whose responsibility is it? If it's you, you need to get your head straight. If it's someone else, you need to get the right people. Spotting the wrong people is equally important. Jargon, cliché and fuzzy language are all enemies of the crucial question: Who is actually going to do this?*

What *Who?* means

Who? is very specific. It means which person? You can't get much clearer than that, and yet frequently it is unclear in business who is supposed to be doing what. How does this happen? All sorts of static gets in the way of clear communication, much of which can lead to lack of clarity, and breed confusion. Sometimes, a meeting will agree the broad principle of something, but fail to work out who precisely is going to do it. Other times, people make the fatal mistake of writing down more than one person as the ones who will do the thing in question, thereby allowing each to assume the other will do it. Sometimes someone agrees to do something, and then doesn't. One way or another, it's an unholy mess that needs disentangling. But before we start, let's have a quick look at our obsession with *Who?*

The cult of *Who?*

The human race has been obsessed with the *Who?* question for thousands of years. Who is the king? Who is the pauper? Who is the pillar of justice? Who is the villain? Who are you, sir? Are you to be respected, or vilified? Who's who? In modern times, this has translated into the cult of the celebrity. There are now billion-pound industries built around tracking who does what, where, and with whom.

Millions of people live their lives vicariously through the activities of others. And then they copy them. What they wear. How they cut their hair. Whether they have tattoos in certain places. Even the places they have dinner, if they can afford it. There are many books that chronicle this strange phenomenon, but the best, in my opinion, is *Herd* by Mark Earls (subtitled *How to change mass behaviour by harnessing our true nature*). What it basically says is that, whilst there is much talk these days about individual choice and one-to-one marketing, in fact most people simply copy other people. There is a summary in the Appendix.

> *"Everybody hates the way they look, but no one complains about their brain."*
>
> **Old Jewish saying**

The brain is a strange thing. Why would it lead us to be more interested in what someone else is doing than what we are doing ourselves? Suffice to say, our obsession with *Who?* lies at the root of politics, jealousy, rivalry, status, and a whole range of other unhelpful emotions that have the power to destabilize even the most straightforward project.

The power of *Who?*

Okay, let's get down to detail about what can be achieved by using the *Who?* question. Deployed correctly, it can get right to the heart of whether anything is really going to happen. It is a close ally of *How?*, but obviously far more personal, because it has a direct bearing on individuals. If there is nobody present who can do it, then it stands to reason that it probably won't get done. It is also a crucial question for the sole trader, because if you can't do it yourself, then you either need outside help, or the idea is not a runner. If you work on your own, look carefully at the internal *Who?* questions that come a bit later. Whatever your role, bear in mind that clarity and honesty are absolutely essential when you answer them.

How to use the *Who?* question

The *Who?* question forces people to agree that they personally are going to do something, or to accept that someone else is doing it. Assuming you have overcome the *So what?*, *Why?*, and *How?* hurdles, we just want to know *who* is going to do it. Easier said than done? Try some of these questions.

External *Who?* questions

Line of inquiry	Possible answer(s)
Who do we have at our disposal?	(a) Any of 100 people (b) There is only one person who can (c) No one – we're stuffed
Who is going to do this?	(a) Dave (b) Gemma (decide who)
Who is capable of doing this?	(a) Rod (b) Me (c) Both of us
Who is prepared to lead this thing?	(a) Rod (or is he?) (b) Me (see internal questions)
Who is actually prepared to do all the work?	(a) Not Rod (b) Not me (in which case, start again)
Who can we trust to do this?	(a) Not Rod (b) Not me (in which case, start again)

A number of issues are raised here. There are huge differences between who we have at our disposal, and who is the most appropriate person to use. Don't make the basic mistake of grabbing the nearest available person and diving into the job. They may be totally wrong for it (see later: Spotting the wrong people).

Then there is the small matter of capability. There may be various candidates for the role, and let's assume they are all capable of it. Being capable doesn't mean they'll make a good job of it. They may not be prepared to do it, for all sorts of reasons. They may not want to lead the project, or take a role in it, or even to do the work. They might genuinely be too busy. Or a bit of a shirker. Or, dare I say it, a bit untrustworthy. Trust is a strange business, and very hard to put your finger on. But if you have any previous evidence, or even a hunch, that someone won't get the job done, then don't ask them to do it. Whatever the reason, if you believe that they might not do it, then don't get them involved if you can possibly help it.

Internal *Who?* questions

Now let's look at how you might deploy the *Who?* question on yourself. The most likely circumstances are that you are self-employed, and so have to sort everything out yourself. Self-employed delegation is not as oxymoronic as it sounds. Millions of sole traders these days operate virtual networks where they can call on "outside" help, and all of them have suppliers in one way or another. So they have to go through exactly the same thought process when a project needs to get done as employed people do. The answer to the *Who?* question for them may not actually be *me*.

Equally, you may work in a company, but be in a position where the decision rests with you, in which case, a number of internal questions before you discuss it with the team, or tell them who's doing what, may well be time very well spent. Rather than repeat all of the external questions above (some of which may well be relevant), concentrate mainly on the three below. Work out whether you can lead the project (but not actually do it), whether you can actually do it yourself, and then double-check to see if you have deluded yourself.

Line of inquiry	Possible answer(s)
Who is going to lead this?	(a) It's me, and that's fine (b) It can't be me – it's not fine
Who is going to do this?	(a) It's me, and that's fine (b) It can't be me – it's not fine
Is it me? Oh @%!!, what if it's me?	(a) I'm still fine to do it (b) On reflection, it's not fine so I need a plan B

Ask the questions, and fill in your own answers. Question three is arguably the most important, precisely because it is a sense-check for the previous two. Too many people embark on projects having claimed that they are happy to lead or fulfil them, only to discover later that they aren't going to get it done. (For a selection of reasons as to why this might be the case, look at the next section.) So keep asking the question until you are convinced of the answer.

Line of inquiry	Possible answer(s)
_____	_____
_____	_____
_____	_____
_____	_____

Who? **Which person?**

We have established that *Who?* means which person, so let's scrutinize further who that might be. Whenever it is agreed that something must be done, there is always an anxious exchange of glances around the room. We all agree it's a good idea, so who's going to do it? Occasionally, someone volunteers. They might be a genuinely wonderful person. They might have the right skills, they might not. They might really fancy the task because they instinctively know what to do. They might want to do it because they haven't done it before and want to learn. They might want the glory if it goes well. (Nothing in particular wrong with that, but beware the naked glory seekers – there is usually a disaster waiting just around the corner.)

> *"Always beware of the man who says he is not seeking office for himself, for he is the vainest of the lot."*
>
> **Robert Harris**

There are scores of possible reasons. More likely though, is the scene where everybody tries to fob it off on someone else. Why do they do it? There are lots of reasons why this might be the case.

1. People are essentially lazy. They will take every opportunity to do as little as possible for the money they can get away with.
2. Many people are under-confident and do not believe they can do the task.
3. Most people are frightened by change, so they won't put themselves forward because they want to stay in their comfort zone.
4. People are always "too busy" to take the job on, apparently.

Some of these reasons are more valid than others. Being lazy is useless and pointless, in both a personal and company sense. Lazy people think they are being clever, because they are "getting away with it". What they fail to realize is:

(a) Everyone else can see it, and the supposed benefits of not pulling your weight don't last very long.
(b) On a personal level, the only losers are the lazy people themselves, because, as well as doing nothing for anyone else, they don't do anything for themselves either.

Ultimately in life, nothing really happens unless you do it yourself. Or at least, you put the effort in somewhere and results and rewards follow. So laziness is not a helpful trait.

Under-confidence is excusable, but not a long-term position. Everybody has to start somewhere, and do something for the first time. Everyone in the world, even the most senior and the most brilliant, had to start as an apprentice or trainee.

> "I am always doing things I can't do. That's how I get to do them."
>
> **Pablo Picasso**

Being scared of change is no great sin either. We all suffer from it. But the older you get, and the more you try, the more you learn that doing new things is the whole point. Without the challenge, you will end up doing the same thing for years on end in the same old boring job. Not only will you be bored out of your mind, but also it is very likely that your employer will begin to take you for granted and regard you as part of the wallpaper – hardly the ideal circumstances for stimulation or personal advancement.

Who me? I'm too busy

Which brings us to the old chestnut of being "too busy". Oh dear, where do we start with this hoary old excuse? I touched on the phenomenon in *Teach Yourself Running Your Own Business* under the heading: Never cancel a new business meeting because you are "too busy" (p. 31), and again in *Teach Yourself Growing Your Business*: Business does not mean being busy (p. 142). Since this problem never goes away, it requires constant scrutiny and analysis.

> *"Managing directors are not paid to be busy, they are paid to think."*
>
> **Sir Kenneth Cork**

Senior people in companies should rarely be busy. Think about it. They are paid a lot and, in theory, they should be able to dictate what goes into their diary. They should be available regularly to meet their staff and customers, and they should be smart enough to solve tricky issues that arise. If they don't, they shouldn't be there. In order to fulfil these duties, they should therefore be, in the broadest sense, available.

Now let's look at middle management. Why should they be so busy? They have teams of people to do stuff. So, assuming they have made a reasonable fist of working out who should be doing what, they shouldn't be too busy either. They should be calmly administrating things and making sure they happen in an orderly fashion.

> "Sometimes it takes a very clever person to do something unbelievably stupid."
>
> **Old saying**

Which leaves the poor subordinate at the bottom of the pile to sweep up all the nasty stuff. Unless, of course, they have got into the habit of fending off those myriad requests with the sorts of questions that this book recommends: *So what?*, *Why?*, *How?*, and so on.

Stripped down to basics, there are only two reasons why everyone is, apparently, "too busy".

1. The company is incompetent, and inadvisably takes on work that it does not have the resources to deliver.
2. The people are incompetent, and are incapable of doing perfectly reasonable tasks in an orderly fashion without melting down.

Sometimes, it's a bit of both. It is not the role of this book to examine work inefficiencies in detail, but suffice to say it lies at the root of the *Who?* question. Just make sure that, wherever possible, sensible people with a good grip on what they are up to are the ones who are charged with getting the job done.

Who? Which persons?

Actually, it gets worse. Just when we have all heaved a sigh of relief because someone else has taken on the task, we realize there has been a dreadful mistake.

Q. *What is the most common reason for something in business not happening?*
A. *More than one person was charged with doing it.*

Ah yes, the old "joint responsibility" trap. What appears above is not, contrary to what you might have thought, an old gag from the world of commerce. It's not supposed to be a joke, even if it has become one. It is basically what goes on millions of times a day in most companies. Picture the scene. Geoff and Jane have agreed to handle Project Armadillo. Everyone else is delighted because they don't have to do it. Geoff is delighted because he knows Jane is diligent so she'll do it. Jane is happy because she knows that Geoff hasn't got much on at the moment, so he will clearly sort it out. Three months later, Project Armadillo hasn't happened. It's all so predictable.

> *"It is amazing what you can accomplish if you do not care who gets the credit."*
>
> **President Harry S. Truman**

And the moral of the story? Only one person should ever be responsible for something. This is all the more true if one takes ego out of the equation (easier said than done!). Teams who keep ego to a minimum can achieve wonderful things, with very little stress, because everyone is respecting their colleagues and just getting on with it. It's a rare thing. Read on.

The kids are alright

Okay, okay, so obviously if the project is a monster, then the entire thing isn't going to be done by just the one individual. And that's where we get into the whole dreaded area of... yes, you've guessed it, teamwork. Picking a team is a nasty business, and fraught with obstacles. The first is whether the people at your disposal are any good. There is no point in just grabbing the nearest available piece of manpower and charging off towards your deadline.

Whoever: 1. Any person. 2. No matter who. 3. An unknown or unspecified person.

From time to time I am asked by clients why a certain department or function in their business isn't working well. On several occasions, I have been forced eventually to ask them this question:

Have you considered that some of your people may actually be incompetent?

This is a deeply unfashionable question, and in many countries these days, quite possibly illegal. But, since I am not employed by anyone, I can't be fired. Call me old-fashioned, but I can't see anything wrong with looking at a task, looking at the available people, and concluding that some of them can't actually do the job. Now clearly, if you work for a corporation and are putting a team together, then you don't want to cause employment law mayhem. But you can certainly sit down for a short while and work out who can best get the job done. Do not grab the nearest person. Get the best. And if you conclude that they aren't available, then look outside the company or cancel the project.

Whose responsibility?

> *"Bureaucracy, the rule of no one, has become the modern form of despotism."*
>
> **Mary McCarthy**

Let's say you are in charge of the project. The buck stops with you, and that's clear. But you also need to know specifically who is responsible for what in the bowels and deep recesses of the project. There is a trend these days to call this project architecture. Mmm. That sounds to me like the sort of waffle that was invented by management consultancies in order to charge massive fees for not a lot. For a full rundown on this sort of behaviour, read *Dangerous Company* by James O'Shea and Charles Madigan. There is a summary in the Appendix. But for now, let's keep the language simple and stick to simple questions like: Who exactly is doing this?

A good way to map this out is to follow the style of the old trade unions, and generate a who-does-what. Simple, but effective. Don't design it with layers and layers of hierarchy or built-in bureaucracy. That won't help to get the job done.

Who-does-what: relating to the separation of kinds of work performed by different trade unions.

Those of you who love massive spreadsheets to make you feel more powerful may find this a bit surprising, but I can assure you that it works. At the risk of repeating myself, why make something more complicated than it is? Go on, have a go. Just fill in this simple form for your project.

Who-does-what: Project Armadillo
Specific task: _____
Who is doing it: _____
Specific task: _____
Who is doing it: _____

When doing this exercise, do not pre-judge who will like doing what. There are many things that you hate doing that other people quite enjoy, and vice versa. Everybody has their different preferences, and different strengths, so there is no point in second guessing what will work well.

> *"The self-fulfilment of a mouse is not always compatible with the self-fulfilment of a cat."*
>
> **John Gross**

If it's you, get your head straight

Getting your head straight from the outset is critical to being effective. The project or task won't work if you don't think it is going to, or if everyone else thinks it will fail. You have to be positive. Being positive cures almost any difficulty, so long as it does not manifest itself as naivety or blind faith.

> *"A positive attitude may not solve all your problems, but it will annoy enough people to make it worth the effort."*
>
> **Herm Allbright**

Relentless enthusiasm is also an excellent force field. Use it to shield yourself from the detractors and resistor types we encountered in the last chapter.

Who are you?

Knowing what you are all about and emanating that style is essential to leading a project. What am I like? What am I good at? How do I want things done? These are all crucial questions that you need to have answered in private before stamping your mark on the matter in hand. Your team can't take a lead from you if you're not providing a style and a direction. If you are having any difficulties deciding what these qualities should be, try the exercises in *Teach Yourself Growing Your Business* called What am I like? and Decide your own style (p. 127).

If it's someone else, get the people right

It all centres around involving the right people. Curmudgeons, depressives, eeyores and idea-killers have no place in a successful project team. We are looking for a balanced view, so people who wish to express their views are more than welcome, but they must be able to do so in a spirit of cooperation and forward motion. For example, Finance Directors are welcome to express financial constraints, but not if they simply naysay every possibility that the team generates. The same goes for production experts who know technical detail, and who only use their knowledge to neuter new ideas. What cannot be tolerated is someone who constantly bangs on about the past, or who simply sits in the corner saying something along the lines of *"That'll never work"*. Get these characters out of the mix straightaway, or don't select them in the first place.

> *"Stupidity is not the monopoly of the stupid."*
>
> **Kevin Myers**

The team should include people who are prepared to hear a point, add their own observations, and drop out of that element of the discussion if their polarized view does not hold sway. Unduly stubborn people should not be allowed. Nor should bores or loud, strident people who love holding court. These people are usually incapable of self-editing. As the quote says, supposedly bright people are capable of being monumentally stupid given the right conditions, so don't provide those conditions.

> *"People who know the least shout loudest."*
>
> **Ernst Anderson**

You also need to keep an eye on what qualitative researchers call the "bandwagon effect". The bandwagon effect occurs when the view of the loudest person holds sway in any given conversation. Just because somebody is overbearingly dominant does not mean that their view is the most appropriate. So keep an eye on the bullies and crashing bores who try to railroad a view through and foist it on the team. They are frequently wrong, and need to be told, or excluded from the proceedings altogether.

Spotting the wrong people

It takes experience and a keen eye. Ask around. Keep your ears and eyes open. Bad people do pick up a reputation quite quickly. But equally, don't be biased and hold grudges. Soak up the information. Work out what you need, and who might fit the bill. Find out if they are available. Pull a few strings. And make sure you do not involve the wrong ones.

There are no hard and fast rules, but there are some basics that dictate whether the mix of people you have chosen are likely to make the project a success. Determining who is *not* right for it is a reasonable way of working this out. Broadly speaking, things will not work if:

- People are dishonest.
- Anybody pulls rank.
- People already think they know the answer.

- People dig in with their preconceived view and refuse to budge.
- Anyone holds a grudge.
- Anyone is prone to talking nonsense.
- Anyone is addicted to the use of jargon (see next).

This list is not exhaustive. Take the time to consider the characteristics of those you wish to involve. If they have these types of qualities, do not invite them to join in because they will not help solve the problem.

Jargon and cliché red alert

Those who are addicted to jargon have become so pervasive in business that they deserve special attention, so that you can learn how to avoid them whenever possible. It's everywhere now. Politicians, newsreaders, Americans, and journalists started it, and now business has thoroughly embraced it.

> *"Clichés are the crutches of the emotionally crippled."*
> **Spike Milligan**

Business does not work if people talk nonsense, use too many acronyms or are wedded to the use of jargon. Only plain English will do. Over the years, I have collected as many of these appalling phrases as I can, but frankly it's hard work keeping pace. As far as I am concerned, all the words and phrases in the Cliché and Jargon Red Alert List below are banned. You can also add your own, particularly if you work in an industry where jargon is the norm. These words are banned for the simple reason that they always limit clear expression and prevent people from articulating what they really mean.

Have fun by haranguing people who talk this sort of rubbish!

> *"Let's have some new clichés."*
>
> **Samuel Goldwyn**

CLICHÉ AND JARGON RED ALERT LIST

(Add your own over time)

Right across the board	There are no easy answers
Play a vital part	Key/key drivers
Any word attached to -driven (e.g. customer-driven)	Cold, hard facts
Take a long hard look	Overviews and scenarios
Acid test	Frameworks
State of the art	Cutting or leading edge
Cut through	Step change
Paradigm shift	Hit the ground running
Going forward	Silver bullet
Multiple core objectives (there is only one core)	DNA
A raft of proposals	B2B or B2C
Benchmark	Best practice
Core competencies	Teeing up
Missions and tasks/mission critical	Holistic
Empowerment/enablement	Give it traction
Get into bed with	Fast-track
Anything to do with focus	Offline
Singing from the same hymn sheet	Deliverables
Go for the low hanging fruit	Leverage

Inputs (especially as a verb)	Touch base
Any artificial -ize verb (optimize, diarize, priorize)	No-brainer
Thinking outside the box	No stone unturned
Pushing the envelope	Take this offline
Innovative	By the end of play
Proactive	Ballpark figures
Seamless	There's no "I" in team
Stakeholder	Get our ducks in a row
Synergy	It's not rocket science
Ring fenced	Bottom line
At the end of the day	Win–win
24/7/365	Umbrella
Wash its own face	Added value

If you are convening a meeting, particularly if it is a dreaded brainstorm, circulate this list beforehand and have some fun in the session by fining anyone who talks this type of rubbish.

> *"It's better to be quotable than honest."*
>
> **Tom Stoppard**

Who's next?

If someone is good at something, then use them again and again. If you have a gem of a colleague or an employee who is brilliant at a particular thing, then deploy them often on that type of work. Obviously you need to keep an eye on whether they ultimately get bored of doing it, but as long as you praise them for their good work and ask them reasonably often if they enjoy it, then things should be alright.

Who by numbers

A word of caution about systems, processes and procedures – basically, anything that falls back on the numbers, the dates, the structures, and the non-human elements of a job that needs to be done. There's absolutely nothing wrong with having a clear process. But be careful if it becomes the overriding point of a project, rather than the original objective, or the views of intelligent people who are doing it. The numbers and the process aren't the main point. The endgame and the people are.

Won't get fooled again

A short word, too, about learning from what has gone on before. As the years go by, you will pick up a lot about how projects work, and who does them well. If things have gone horribly wrong before, then try to equate that with what may go wrong again, and head it off before it does actually happen. Don't repeat the mistakes you made before, and don't create the conditions that make them more likely. It's agonizing to watch the same calamity unfold in the same business year after year. Don't be one of those people who never learn. Get the *Who?* right and your efforts should proceed much more smoothly.

Summary of *Who?* thinking

1. *Who?* means what person?
2. Use the *Who?* question to be very specific about who is doing something.

3. Address external *Who?* questions to colleagues.
4. Address internal *Who?* questions to yourself.
5. Be suspicious of people who claim to be too busy.
6. Think carefully about the composition of teams.
7. Distinguish between responsibility and action.
8. If it's you who has to do the leading or working, get your head straight.
9. Learn how to spot the wrong people.
10. If people are good at something, use them again and again.

Exercise: Who is actually going to do this?

1. Set out the project or task on the table and ponder the implications. Work out whether this is a job for an individual or a team. If it is an individual, is it you or someone else?

2. If it is you, cross-examine yourself to make absolutely sure that you have the skills, and the desire to do it. If not, reconsider. If it is someone else, think about who it should be and why.

3. Plan how to approach that person and generate a plan B in case they say no.

4. If it is a team, write down all the necessary things that need to get done, and put a name by each of them. Keep the number of names as low as possible. Work through all the people and all the tasks until you have as tightknit a gang as possible.

5. Now go and talk to them all to see if your plan can indeed become reality.

When?

This chapter covers what When? *means. At what time? Over what period? Understanding the time spectrum is essential to getting things done. In some cases it's now or never. In others, long-, medium-, short-, and no-term possibilities need to be examined. Dealing with deadlines is aided by introducing the concept of livelines. If you are going to panic, then learn how to panic early. Essay crises don't work, and problems are better handled in bite-sized chunks. Anticipate time lags and learn what to do about them.*

The power of *When?*

When? causes little offence when spoken, but conceals the time bomb waiting to go off with any task. You have agreed that something is a great idea. You know why it is happening, and you have decided how it will get done, and who is going to do it. Sounds straightforward enough, doesn't it? But when *exactly* will the job be done? The power of *When?* is that it immediately sorts out good intentions from actuality, and helps you to get things in the right order of priority. (I refuse to say priorize or prioritize – the first isn't even in the dictionary, and sounds like booking someone into a priory.) *When?* is a killer. It lurks behind deadlines. It causes dread at the end of financial and tax years. It provokes debates on ageism. It forms the whole basis of our timing system. And yet it sounds so innocent. We will look at lots of these implications in this chapter.

What *When?* means

Precisely what *When?* means is very simple. It has two clear meanings. *At what time?* and *Over what time period?* The two versions can mean hugely different things. *At what time?* seems clear enough. The people involved agree a time and that's when it all happens. We'll discuss lateness and punctuality later, but at least the intention is beyond dispute. If it's three o'clock, then three o'clock it is.

When: 1. At what time? 2. Over what period?

It's with the second definition, *Over what period?*, that most of the havoc occurs. How many projects are actually completed on time? An unanswerable question of course, but the point is made nonetheless. We have all worked on tasks that migrate from being screamingly urgent to relatively unimportant. Millions of tasks are late or never even finished. Why is this? Does it matter? Let's have a look in detail.

When? At what time?

As my old tutor used to say: "Time was invented by man to stop everything happening at once." Time breaks down into units that man has tinkered with from time to time, but never really got right. The Romans so nearly got it spot on. They started with a 10-month year, and then ruined it all by slotting in a couple of extra ones to honour two of their favourite statesmen (Julius and Augustus). So we ended up with a complete hotchpotch of a calendar system that doesn't work particularly well.

Our months are a variety of different lengths, the ninth month is called the seventh, and so on, all the way through to December, and every four years we have to adjust with a leap year because they don't add up anyway. There is no particular pattern as to why we have four weeks in a month, seven days in a week, 24 hours in a day, or 60 minutes in an hour. It's all a bit unsatisfactory, and for over 2000 years no one has been imaginative enough to improve the system. For a complete list of how we have chosen to divide up time and give chunks of it names, look at the Appendix.

Anyway, however confusing the whole system is, it's the one we have to work with. So when someone says "I'll see you at five o'clock for the meeting", at least we know when we are supposed to turn up.

> *"Punctuality is the virtue of the bored."*
>
> **Evelyn Waugh**

Of course, there are those people who are perennially late. I have to say, I am not a fan of such people. They are usually rude, disorganized and, above all, disrespectful of everyone else. They are either so poorly organized that they genuinely don't know where they are supposed to be from one minute to the next, or they arrogantly assume that the world revolves around them. Which of course it doesn't. It shouldn't be beyond the wit of a reasonably sentient being to work out what they need to do, with whom they need to interact, and how much time it might take to arrive at the relevant place in order to do it. Easy, or complicated? It is truly remarkable the number of supposed grown-ups who are perpetually late. Everyone else has to reorganize around them, and they rarely change their ways. For those of you who have to deal with people of this type, I suggest a number of measures.

1. Start the meeting regardless of whether the person has turned up or not, regardless of their seniority.
2. Finish the meeting precisely when it was scheduled, regardless of whether the matter is concluded.

3. Insist on fitting the bits that matter to you into the (truncated) available time.
4. Highlight the shortcomings of the meeting due to their lateness. This may include their failure to hear the full width of a particular debate, inability to deal with enough subject matter, or missed deadlines based on the fact that you will now have to convene at a later date.
5. Keep a note of the number of times they roll in late, and remind them of it on every subsequent occasion until it becomes a source of embarrassment.
6. If they pay no heed, draw up a chart itemizing the effect of their inefficiency on the business.

One way or another, you have to keep going with these people. They cannot be allowed to wander about expecting everybody else to adjust around them. They are just not important enough.

When? Over what period?

Boss: *"How long will it take you to write that report?"*
Employee: *"Three hours."*
Boss: *"Great. I'll see you in three hours then."*

Oh dear. That conversation didn't go too well. The employee fell into the massive trap of defining precisely how long a particular task would take, *in its own right*, without any reference to the broader context of when they might actually be able to start it. This highlights one of the two major problems with the *Over what period?* part of the *When?* question.

Problem 1: Other stuff

No one item, in its own right, is insurmountable or unreasonable to do. It just depends how many of them there are. If there are one or two, then you will probably be able to deliver them in time. If there are an overwhelming number, then maybe not. This component of *When?* is crucial to have a handle on if you are to make a success of getting stuff done effectively and on time.

Problem 2: Vagueness

Most timings are subject to very vague definitions, such as "next week", "next month", or "in quarter two", leading to significant confusion and, usually, slippage. If you are in charge of a project, or if the timing matters a lot to you personally, then do not allow this kind of loose language to pass for precision. If it is not precise, then you can bet your boots that whatever is being asked for will be late. "Next week", for example, will always mean Friday. Tomorrow will mean at the very end of the working day. And any items requested for the next quarter, or any other dim and distant landmark somewhere in the future, probably won't happen at all. It's all in the language, and it's all about deploying the *When?* question judiciously, and making sure you receive accurate and acceptable answers.

How to use the *When?* question

The *When?* question should be used to create clarity. You'll either want to know at what time something is going to happen, or over what time period. If it's just a series of things happening at specific times, then fixing them should be a simple administrative task, and you may well be able to delegate it. Look carefully though at who is required to do what by these times. If their tasks are easy to fulfil, then you'll have no trouble with them arriving at the right time with the right stuff completed. However, if you, or some other pressure, is unrealistically imposing timing that others do not wish to adhere to, then you need to consider whether the proposed deadline is realistic. If, on reflection, it isn't, then change it.

The time period angle of the question is much more fraught. If it is your job to assess how long somebody needs to do something, you need to apply a mixture of technical knowledge and experience of the individual. One school of thought recommends that you put people under pressure and they deliver better. Another says they will rebel against such draconian measures and do worse work. No universal rule applies – you need to work it out for yourself depending on your circumstances. (See later in this chapter: *Why essay crises don't work.*)

External *When?* questions

First of all, try asking these questions of colleagues, customers, and yourself, where relevant.

Line of inquiry	Possible answer(s)
(By) when is this thing needed?	(a) In one hour (b) Tomorrow at 3pm (c) April 30th
When (over what period) will the work be done?	(a) Eight hours (b) Twelve weeks (c) The weekend
When (at what frequency) shall we meet?	(a) Every three hours (b) Every day (c) Every week
When (at what time) shall we meet?	(a) At 10am, 1pm, and 4pm (b) At 9am every morning (c) At 11am every Friday

Be as precise as you can. The more vague the answer, the more likely it is that the thing will be late, and the less likely it is that the thing will be done at all.

Internal *When?* questions

If things are getting bogged down, or if you work for yourself, you may need to take a quiet moment to cross-examine yourself. Try these.

(By) when does this have to be done?	(a) In one hour (b) Tomorrow at 3pm (c) April 30th
When exactly am I going to do it?	(a) Between 2 and 3pm (b) Tuesday 9–11am (c) Every Monday this month
(By) when do I need someone else to do this?	(a) In one hour (b) Tomorrow at 3pm (c) April 30th
When (over what period) will they do it?	(a) Between 2 and 3pm (b) Tuesday 9–11am (c) Every Monday this month

Understanding the time spectrum

To get a proper grip on when things may or may not get done, you need to understand the time spectrum. This will help you put things in a sensible order of priority, and work out how important they really are.

> *"If you're planning for one year, plant rice. If you're planning for ten years, plant trees. If you're planning for 100 years, educate people."*
>
> **Chinese proverb**

The proverb sums it up well. Small things can be knocked over fast, and require only simple approaches. Longer-term plans require more complicated solutions, and a lot more thought. The really big stuff may well require way more than tools and approaches. It may call for a whole new way of doing something, complete with the understanding of a team who currently have no knowledge of the long-term goal or how to get there.

The time spectrum needn't be complex. At one end is now. At the other end is never, or so far away as to be irrelevant or unhelpful. Scarily, everything else falls somewhere in the middle, and that's where it can go horribly wrong.

It's now or never

Let's break it down simplistically first, for the avoidance of all doubt. If something is really easy, do it now. What is now? Well, if you work on your own and control your working life, do it literally *now*. If you are employed by someone else but have a high degree of autonomy, then you should also aim to do it right now. If you work in a company and have a fair bit to do, then work out how quickly "now" can be. Have a look at these definitions to decide which suit you best.

Possible definitions of now:
- This second.
- Within the next minute.
- Within the next five minutes.
- Within the hour.
- Definitely this morning.
- Definitely this afternoon.
- Definitely today.

I am trying to be reasonable here. One person's definition of "now" is not the same as another's. However, as a rough rule of thumb, I would suggest that "now" should never be further off than today. If you are the sort of person who fundamentally disagrees with this, I have two suggestions:

1. Get a grip. You have obviously cornered the market in prevarication, and are an irritation to all your colleagues (or yourself if you are self-employed).
2. Throw this book away. There is little I can pass on that you will agree with, so let's agree to disagree.

> *"Death and taxes and childbirth. There's never a convenient time for any of them."*
>
> **Margaret Mitchell**

Understanding time

Understanding how time works in your particular business is crucial to knowing when things will get done, and whether they actually stand a chance of getting done at all. This is such a fine line. Millions of people rush about in business labouring under the massive misapprehension that everything *will* happen, and that it's just a matter of *when.* Experience suggests that this is nonsense – a huge proportion of the stuff on anyone's "To Do" list will *never actually happen.*

This is a brutal fact that you must face head on if you are to make any sensible progress with increasing the likelihood of things happening. Get the *When?* questions sorted out early on, and the ratio of things getting done will rise massively.

Long-, medium-, short-, and no-term

Of course, it isn't realistic for a book to dictate exactly what your time bands will look like, but we can map out some broad parameters. We have already established that the time spectrum has *now* at one end, and *never* at the other. Let's be mature about it and admit that now means sometime very soon, as defined by the list we have just looked at. Equally, let's agree that for lots of things, the answer to the question "*When will this be done?*" is, sadly, never. Both of these extremes are essentially no-term options, because one happens straightaway, and the other never happens at all. Excluding the no-term options is an excellent way of removing unrealistic tasks, and quick, easy-to-do ones, from your list. (This elimination process is a close cousin of Establish how not to do it in Chapter 3.)

So, instead let's examine the nasty ragbag of stuff that falls on the line in between now and never. The words have been somewhat overused, but let's try for a moment to work with them and divide the tasks into long-term, medium-term, and short-term. Once again, we have to sort out the definitions of these, because they will vary hugely by the nature of the business you are in. Here are some differences.

Newspaper industry

Definition of short-term:	In the next five minutes
Definition of medium-term:	In one hour
Definition of long-term:	By tonight

Home delivery of consumer durables

Definition of short-term:	In the next two days
Definition of medium-term:	In the next week
Definition of long-term:	By next month

Car manufacturing

Definition of short-term: In the next month
Definition of medium-term: In one year
Definition of long-term: Within five years

Confusing, isn't it? They are all using the same words, but they don't mean the same thing. This is where it all starts to fall down. My use of the phrase "short-term" may not be the same as yours. So it pays to use language that is much more precise, so that everybody knows what is being asked for, and when it really needs to be done. Always ask for answers to the *When?* question in absolute terms, particularly if you are new to a company or a sector. You may agree to a "short-term" timing and get a shock when you discover that they meant by tea time.

Dealing with deadlines

So this is where we have to grapple with the thorny issue of deadlines. The dictionary reveals little about the origin of why they are called deadlines, and simply describes them as a "time limit for any activity". Indeed, beyond this point, presumably, there should be no activity because the issue is, effectively, dead. But that's not how it works in reality. Deadlines come and go all the time, and they usually aren't met.

> *"I love deadlines. I like the whooshing sound they make as they fly by."*
>
> **Douglas Adams**

Introducing livelines

The biggest mistake that everybody makes when dealing with deadlines is to concentrate on the deadline rather than

LIVELINES AND DEADLINES

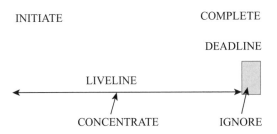

Fig. 5.1: Livelines and deadlines

the bit that comes before. This is kindergarten stuff, and yet there's not a business in the world that doesn't suffer from it. To repeat: *the bit at the end is irrelevant, it's what you do beforehand that matters.* This is so basic as to sound almost insulting. So why is it then that companies and individuals always leave everything to the last minute? In my training schemes, I must have heard every excuse in the book. The old chestnut of "being too busy" is usually trotted out. "Work pressure" is often cited (often by those in charge, who could actually dictate the pace themselves!). But the most self-deluding of all is the old cliché: "I work better under pressure." This is total nonsense, as we shall see in a moment.

So it's time to start ignoring the deadline, and start concentrating on the liveline, the period of time that comes before it (see Figure 5.1). After all, this is where all the work gets done, and it should be 99% longer than the deadline.

How long is a deadline?

This may sound like a daft question, but it isn't. If you think about it, the length of a deadline is directly related to the length of the project. Here are some examples.

Length of project	Length of deadline ("Moment of launch")
One hour	One minute
One day	Five minutes
One week	Twenty minutes
One month	Half an hour
Three months	One hour
One year	Half a day
Five years	One day

In other words, the length of the project will determine the window allowed to announce that it is finished, and of course, the length of time needed to explain to all and sundry that it is finished, and what it means. It only takes a couple of minutes to read a hundred words explaining the achievement of a one-hour exercise, but most of the day for the Chancellor to explain the contents of an annual budget. You get the idea. So once you have allocated the deadline, don't spend any more time concentrating on it. Initiate the project, and spend all your time concentrating on the liveline that constitutes 99% of the work required.

If you're going to panic, learn how to panic early

If there is a lesson to be learned from this new focus, it is that, if you are going to panic, then do it early. In other words, put the frenetic activity in early on,

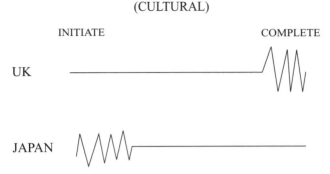

Fig. 5.2: Dealing with deadlines: cultural

so that there is plenty of time to make mistakes, and rectify them. Different cultures approach deadlines in different ways. Figure 5.2 shows a hypothetical time line for the launch of a product being manufactured and marketed by the Japanese and the British. It should be self-explanatory, but for the avoidance of doubt, the Japanese are more likely to have their problems early, with the British panicking at the last moment. In your opinion, national pride or xenophobia aside, who do you think is the more likely to produce an excellent product on time?

Why essay crises don't work

So let's return to the cliché: "I work better under pressure." This assertion is based loosely on the unspoken conspiracy between all students at college, roughly translated as: "I do barely any work for the whole week, spend vast amounts of time in the pub, and then cram a shoddy last-minute attempt into the last few (usually small) hours." These

APPROACHING A DEADLINE
(PERSONAL)

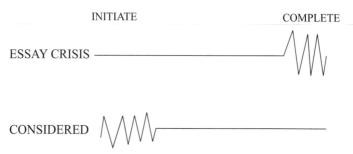

Fig. 5.3: Dealing with deadlines: personal

people then carry on like this in their business lives, thinking that it is acceptable behaviour. It doesn't work, for lots of reasons.

1. Being a natural prevaricator, you get that familiar horrible sinking feeling when you know you have to deliver to a deadline.
2. This feeling persists for the entire period that you fail to do the necessary work, thereby effectively creating a monkey on your back the majority of the time.
3. If something else unexpected crops up, you have no room for manoeuvre in which to cope with it.
4. You have no slippage time in which to make mistakes, pursue lines of inquiry that do not prove fruitful, change your mind, or simply have a better idea.
5. Rushed work is invariably of a lower standard than carefully considered work.
6. If you have more than one project on the go with overlapping time lines, this apparently temporary condition of anxiety will be a permanent state.

So do not persist with the essay crisis model. It doesn't work and it never has.

Bite-sized chunks

As we move towards the end of our look at the *When?* question, there are some useful pieces of advice that may help when you are striving to get things done, or even to plan to get them done. The first is always to break things down into bite-sized chunks. As the old joke goes: *How do you eat an elephant? One mouthful at a time.* Smaller chunks lead to greater clarity and are far less daunting than the full picture. Be quizzical about, and sceptical of, really long-term plans such as 100-day plans. They never happen as predicted. Stick to one-day plans or, at the most, 10-day plans.

If you want the world's simplest mantra for organizing your work, just ask yourself: *Now, what shall I do today?*

Time lags and what to do about them

As a general rule of life, and so business, nothing ever happens when it is supposed to. Sometimes it never happens at all. But most of the time there is simply a time lag between when it was supposed to happen and when it actually does. It pays to recognize this early on in life, and in any given project. Don't get frustrated. Most things are late, and it pays to acknowledge the likelihood before it happens, to avoid disappointment. These time lags and what to do about them are covered in some detail in *Teach Yourself Running Your Own Business*, p. 76.

> *"Days are lost lamenting over lost days. What you can do, or think you can do, begin it."*
>
> **Goethe**

The false metrics of the Finance Director

Time lags are one thing, but blatant false predictions are another. Be very wary of financial forecasts, because they never happen as predicted. Every year, flying in the face of all previous wisdom, Finance Directors produce forecasts that bear no relation to reality at all. If things don't go as the spreadsheet suggested at the beginning of the year, they have a number of tricks up their sleeve to adjust everything. These include changing the year-end, cross-fiscal juggling, obfuscation of year-on-year comparisons, seasonal adjustments, and regular forecast revisions.

Companies really should know better by now. Every year they know that their year plan won't work, but every year they carry on and predict it anyway. Why is this? Is it because businesses are populated by greedy, dim executives who aren't clever enough to approach it any other way? Or because no one has properly debated the way in which we deliberately distort time to avoid facing the things that really matter?

Whatever the reasons, as Finance Directors all over the world massively miss the point when making their business forecasts, make sure that you don't get caught up in the chaos. Every year their false metrics manage to convince the business (and themselves) that everything will proceed in an orderly fashion, which, of course, it never does. Leave them to it, by all means, but don't believe it yourself.

Timing your run

Choosing when to time your run with a boss, colleague, customer, or department needs a little bit of careful thought. If at all possible, try to work out when a crucial decision might be required long before it becomes critical or horribly time-sensitive. This will help to take the pressure off everyone involved, and keep everybody calm. Some chance! No seriously, by considering the possibility of a crisis in the near future, you can usually avoid one. Time your run judiciously:

- When there is a big, tricky issue to sort out.
- When there is no agreement on something and that is blocking progress.
- When something has been hanging around for ages without resolution.

Stay calm though. The circumstances may be pressurized, but that does not mean that you need to be.

When did this happen before?

If something looks nasty, or possibly insurmountable, consider the value of history. By which I mean, ask the question: *When did this happen before?* Obviously, if it never has (in the experience of you or the company), then there is nothing to be learnt. But that is fairly rare in business, and there is usually some prior knowledge that can be accessed to help the current situation. Ask around and see who knows what. Draw together any past learning and see if it is relevant to the present. Equally, do not fall into the trap of thinking that, just because something worked before, it will do so again (or vice versa). Things change, and you need to too.

When will I see you again?

Regular reviews, although fairly dull and predictable, are a good way of avoiding nasty surprises, or at least getting earlier warning of them. I am not a fan of routine, but if you keep asking *When?* throughout the course of a project, you are unlikely to be caught short thinking that something is on course to be delivered on time, when actually it isn't.

> *"A lifetime commitment – man, that's a hell of a lot of breakfasts."*
>
> **Humphrey Bogart on marriage**

Whenever isn't enough

In the same way that a teenager saying "whatever" is irritating, use of the word "whenever" is pointless when determining when something is going to be done. No vagueness is allowed. We established earlier in the chapter the two most common things that blur clarity in this area: 1. Other stuff and 2. Vagueness. Work hard to prevent these from deviating you from your task.

Just say when

Frustrating though it is, sometimes you just have to call time on things that aren't working. It may be one small element of a project, or the entire thing. Look coldly at the facts and then face them head on. If something isn't working, admit it and change it.

Subsidiary *When?* questions

Here are a few subsidiary questions that you may wish to ask to add texture to timing issues:

- What time is it? It's late. No it isn't, it's early.
- Is that so far off that we won't take it seriously?
- When are we going to make some decisions?
- When are we prepared to call it off if it isn't working?
- When is it due?

Summary of *When?* thinking

1. *When?* means: at what time? or over what period?
2. Other stuff and vagueness are its main enemies.
3. Consider external and internal *When?* questions.
4. Understand the time spectrum.
5. If you can do it now, then do it, or it may be never.
6. Long-, medium-, short-, and no-term: beware imprecise language.
7. Deal with livelines, and the deadlines will take care of themselves.
8. If you're going to panic, learn how to panic early.
9. Essay crises don't work.
10. Break tough jobs into bite-sized chunks.
11. Beware time lags and anticipate them.
12. Beware the false metrics of the Finance Director.
13. Time your run carefully.
14. Use history to learn.
15. If something isn't working, change it.

Exercise: When to publicize the plan

1. You have been put in charge of a project, and are now scrutinizing the timing. First of all, write down everything that needs to happen and put them in a sensible order.

2. Pause and consider the likelihood of things going exactly as the plan predicts. Human nature and past experience suggest that they won't. Now build in a healthy amount of time for slippages, mishaps, and unexpected developments.

3. Draft up the plan to provide a rough shape. Now consider all the characters (colleagues, suppliers, bosses, and you) who need to be available to (a) do the work and (b) approve what has been done. Pay particular attention to likely holidays, possible illness, traditional panic phases in the business, and any overlap with other significant projects that are important to the company.

4. Revise the plan based on all the above. Now consider to whom you need to communicate the new plan. Be aware of, and sensitive to, those with a large vested interest in the project. They might be the boss whose future depends on the timing of the project, or the poor souls who have to do most of the work, and who probably have loads of other things to do already.

5. Work out the most appropriate way to break the news to them. Lobby if necessary. Build your case, and make your reasoning clear. When you have informed everyone involved, go public with the plan.

Where?

6

This chapter covers what Where? *means. In, at, or to what place, point, or position? In, at, or to which place? How to get the plan from your head out to the wider world. Dealing with modern virtual teams. Being specific about city, country, and continental involvement. How wherehousing can help problems with multinational teams. Identifying wherewolves and tracking them down. How to play hunt the colleague.*

What *Where?* means

As ever with these small words that we use every day and pretty much take for granted, they can often mean a bit more than we bargained for. *Where?* sounds easy enough, but can mean lots of things.

Where: 1. In, at, or to what place, point, or position?
2. In, at, or to which place?

At first glance, these two definitions look pretty much the same, but the person writing the dictionary wouldn't have bothered to distinguish between the two if they *were* exactly the same, so let's examine the difference. It all revolves around your interpretation of the word "place". It could mean a physical place such as your desk, a room, an office, a city, or a country. These move from the small to the vast. If I say something is on my desk, then you should be able to find it, give or take my degree of tidiness. If I tell you to find something in India, without giving you any more detail than that, then you may have a bit more trouble.

So that's physical place. It can have its complications, depending on scale and the level of detail provided. Mental place is way more complex. If *Where?* refers to a mental position, it may be anything from an idea in my head, to the prevailing opinion in a team, or the views of an entire race or nation, as in: "*Where do you stand on this?*"

As well as the physical/mental distinction, we need to look carefully at whether *Where?* is referring to the static point of something or the desired direction of it, as in *Where are we heading to?* Direction has implied motion, so *Where?* can be dynamic as well as static and specific.

All of these nuances will be investigated in this chapter, but first let's examine what the *Where?* question can achieve.

The power of *Where?*

The *So what?* and the *Why?* questions have helped us to establish the point of a project. *How?* has proved that it can indeed be done, *Who?* has ensured that proper responsibility is being taken for it, and *When?* should have nailed the timing. *Where?* is a close cousin to all of them, and its significance has increased massively in recent years since the onset of the information age, globalization, and the power of the Internet. Thousands of books have been written about this phenomenon, and we will deal with a number of the issues that the almost-instant transfer of information and ideas around the globe raises.

In *The World Is Flat*, Thomas L. Friedman scours the planet to show how knowledge and resources are connecting everywhere as never before. This he describes as the "flattening" of the world, and argues that it can be a force for good in business, for the environment, and for people everywhere. *The Long Tail*, by Chris Anderson, demonstrates the viability of products that can be distributed around the world for a fraction of the price of goods in conventional stores. And *The Cluetrain Manifesto* (Levine, Locke, Searls and Weinberger) explains how ideas can appear all around the world in seconds, so companies need to make very sure that they are not lying, fudging, or in any way being economical with the truth, otherwise they will be exposed by the next day. Summaries of all of these are in the Appendix.

The point is, *Where?* can be a more complicated question than you might think, and these days the answer could lie up to 10,000 miles away, and be just as feasible as the office next door. So, if the question has the capacity to yield a global answer, how shall we apply it?

How to use the *Where?* question

Let's assume that you have sorted all the other questions. You are at the stage where you know why something is being done, how it is going to get done, and who is going to do it. If you are very fortunate, designating who is doing it will also cure the issue of where it is going to be done, but, in this ultra-flexible modern world, maybe not. Time was, you could pull out a large chart, wave a hefty pointer, and prod it whilst proclaiming: "That will be handled by our Romford facility." But as vast proportions of what is "produced" these days is advice and service, the answer could be virtual, or so complicated as to make your head spin.

So the *Where?* question demands answers that are extremely precise. As with the other questions, flabby answers serve little purpose, and render the question near pointless. So if you pose it, demand a clear answer. Also, consider what level of clarity you require before you ask it. Do you need a geographical answer, or a mental one? Are you asking for a specific static location, or a desired direction?

If you, the questioner, are muddled about this, then you will probably receive a fuzzy or evasive response. RIRO: Rubbish In, Rubbish Out, as the old computer programming acronym has it.

Unlike the other chapters, we will not be distinguishing between internal and external *Where?* questions. The reason for this is that, on examination, they all turn out to be pretty much the same. Instead, there is a much more interesting distinction to be had between the physical place *Where?* questions and the mental state *Where?* questions. Read on.

In, at, or to what place, point, or position?

Stripping *Where?* down to its bare bones, the first interpretation we encounter is "in, at, or to what place, point, or position?" That gives us six variables and nine possibilities to look at.

Where question	Possible answer/next question
In what place?	Name a building
At what place?	Name a geographical location
To what place?	Something needs to move from A to B
In what point?	At what stage should it happen?
At what point?	Name the time in the process
To what point?	To which stage in the process?
In what position?	What orientation do we desire?
At what position?	...in relation to everything else?
To what position?	To which new position in the process?

Whoa! Has that done your head in? Who would have thought that such a little question could cause so much havoc and lead to so many more? Don't panic. All we are trying to do is make you think that bit harder about where things will actually get done. Take the time to tease apart the simpler physical answers from the more diffuse mental ones.

In, at, or to which place?

In which place?	A physical or mental one? Specify
At which place?	A physical or mental one? Specify
To which place?	A physical or mental one? Specify

It's all about being specific. Vague answers such as "Department S will handle that one" or "That's one for Chicago" won't help the cause.

The importance of precision

Take a look at these examples to give a flavour of what is an acceptable response, and what is not.

Question: *Where precisely will that idea be generated?*
Acceptable precise answer: *By me.*
Unacceptable vague answer: *We'll have a brainstorm one day.*

Question: *Where precisely will that document be written?*
Acceptable precise answer: *By Steve, on his computer.*
Unacceptable vague answer: *The project team will put something together.*

Question: *Where precisely will that team operate?*
Acceptable precise answer: *On the third floor, by the window.*
Unacceptable vague answer: *Remotely, logging in from time to time.*

Question: *Where precisely will that department work?*
Acceptable precise answer: *In London.*
Unacceptable vague answer: *It's a multi-cultural, multi-centre solution.*

Question: *Where precisely will that office be located?*
Acceptable precise answer: *Number 23 Duncan Street, London.*
Unacceptable vague answer: *Geoff is looking at options as we speak.*

Question: *Where precisely will responsibility lie?*
Acceptable precise answer: *With me.*
Unacceptable vague answer: *The project team have a dotted line into Linda, via Helsinki.*

You get the idea. If the answer is clear, then so are you. If you are clear, then everybody else probably is too.

Where? In your head

Something may be clear in your head, but what happens thereafter? Like Chinese whispers, everything can become distorted, and go peculiar.

Chinese whispers:
1. A game in which a message is passed on, in whisper, so that the final version is often radically changed from the original.
2. Any situation where information is passed on in turn by a number of people, often becoming distorted in the process.

The journey from your head to the wider world is a strange one. We are making the assumption here that you have

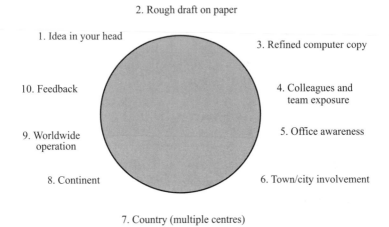

FROM YOUR HEAD TO THE WORLD

2. Rough draft on paper

1. Idea in your head

3. Refined computer copy

10. Feedback

4. Colleagues and
team exposure

9. Worldwide
operation

5. Office awareness

8. Continent

6. Town/city involvement

7. Country (multiple centres)

Fig. 6.1:   From your head to the world

a vision for something, that you need to communicate
something, or that you are in charge and need to disseminate
your leadership direction to others. You have worked out
what you want to do, and how it needs to be done. Now
you have to go public and let everyone else know. Have a
look at the schematic in Figure 6.1 and determine where
you are in the process.

We'll suppose that you are at the beginning. Where the idea
is at this stage is either: (a) in your head or, put another way,
(b) nowhere. As we established in Chapter 3, (The power of
How?), an idea doesn't officially exist until you have executed
it. So vigorous efforts are needed to get it out and about.

Where? Rough draft on paper

Sketched on a napkin. Scribbled on a beer mat. Or on the
back of a fag packet (that's cigarette, for the benefit of our

American readers). Some of the world's best plans were conceived on the humblest materials. I am a great fan of paper, recycled of course. First of all, try to articulate your plan or idea as a rough draft on paper. This will immediately reveal (a) its sheer brilliance or (b) its appalling pitfalls. In truth though, if you have exposed the idea to the rigour of the questions in the previous chapters, it should be pretty good. So we should be able to push it out to the wider world.

Where? Refined computer copy

Naturally, your proposal is ingenious at the conceptual stage. Now you need to make it intelligible and articulate it in a way that is convincing for everyone else that matters to its success.

> *"Madness is a rare thing in individuals, but in groups, parties, peoples and ages, it is the rule."*
>
> **Nietzsche**

It's a funny thing. Apart from extreme weirdos, most people are eminently reasonable when dealt with individually. (I am not a fan of the one-to-one or face-to-face jargon that is so prevalent these days.) A few megalomaniacs will look you dead in the eye and behave like a twit to your face, but they are the exception. (If they are the norm, then leave your company immediately.) And yet, as soon as you put "normal" people in front of others in a business context, they start behaving in most peculiar ways. They don't say what they mean half the time. The other half, they find themselves agreeing with some of the maddest ideas anyone can generate. Ill-conceived brainstorms, showboating, political manoeuvring – whatever the reason, madness can be the rule in groups.

So take your rough idea and find a superlative way of expressing it. Don't settle for hackneyed formats like PowerPoint or lengthy, verbose documents. Find a pithy and engaging medium to give it your best shot. Given the dominance of technology in business today, I have elected to call this the refined computer copy, in deference to the likelihood that it probably will have to reside somewhere on your computer, because some form of electronic version will probably be mandatory. But do try to be as original and thoughtful as you can.

Where? Colleagues and team exposure

So you are going public with your idea, and the answer to the *Where?* question is now migrating from "*my head*" to "*someone else's head*". At this stage we are assuming that colleagues and team exposure is restricted to around about a maximum of 10 people. The first crucial point to grasp is that they might not get it. Don't dive in and assume that they will. We've all been in meetings where, despite lengthy preparation, and supposedly lucid explanation, the other lot just don't get it. Be prepared for this. The simpler and more memorable your articulation, the more likely the chance of their understanding what you are on about.

> "*We don't see things as they are, we see them as we are.*"
>
> **Anais Nin**

Where? Office awareness

You have to get people's attention. Why should they be interested in your stuff? The *Where?* question moves to a wider range now, to encompass all sorts of people who may or may not give a damn about what you think is important, or the value of what you are trying to achieve. Of course, the people at the core, and the ones interested in the money, will be watching you like a hawk. (This expression covers both attention to detail, and range of vision. An eagle has little difficulty in spotting a rabbit a mile away, and it is no coincidence when someone's ability to pay attention is directly related to their vested interest in the subject matter.)

> *"90% of success is showing up."*
>
> **Woody Allen**

Those closely interested in a project tend these days to be called the stakeholders, but the word has been so bastardized in recent years that I am not a fan of it. A true stakeholder must have a direct financial interest or a significant spiritual interest in something, but these days the word is used to convey pretty much any audience. It's too loose, and the context is usually disingenuous, intended to suggest that people's best interests are being well served, when in fact they are not.

If you are announcing something, you need their undivided attention, if only for a short time (the shorter the better). With imagination and good facilitation (by you), this can be done anywhere. The first big hurdle is getting them to turn up. For a bit of drama and novelty, you might want to do it out of the office. Most offices are hideous environments and, no matter how hard people try, they tend to fall into regimented patterns of behaviour in them. They also suffer from the *"I must just pop out and have a word with Nigel"* syndrome. Mobile phones and similar electronic devices need to be physically collected at the front door. If anyone cannot pay attention for the length of the session, then they can't come in, or they need to be physically removed, or you have made it too long and boring.

> *"There is no such thing as an uninteresting subject – only an uninterested student."*
>
> **Old academic saying**

The whole business of persuading the people in your office to go along with something is so important that it deserves a lot of attention. Corporations these days have a nasty habit of calling it buy-in, as in: *"We can't get a green light until we get buy-in from Brian"*, and other such phraseology. In fact, come to think of it, you'd be hard-pushed to watch the news on most evenings without hearing a politician mentioning *"stakeholder buy-in"*. By the time they have extended it to *"key stakeholder buy-in"*, the poor viewer could be forgiven for having a vision of a bloke holding a wooden stake in one hand, and a key in the other, being confronted by someone offering a tempting wedge of cash. It all serves to complicate understanding, so keep the language simple.

Preparation: what *you* have to do beforehand

People will go along with you if you think carefully beforehand about their possible reactions and expectations. Consider these points:

- Choose the right people who are most likely to contribute constructively.

- Choose the right environment.
- Make them prepare (possibly, see next).
- Make sure they understand the rules of engagement (see later).
- Anyone who cannot attend cannot comment.

This last point is vitally important. There is a nasty tendency in modern business for supposedly important people not to turn up to a meeting, and then to overrule its findings or recommendations later on. This is completely out of order. Introduce a "No attendance, no role in the decision making" rule. If they haven't got the good manners to come, then pay no attention to their opinion.

Preparation: what *they* have to do beforehand

In some circumstances, it works well if your audience actually have to prepare before a meeting or announcement, as well as you. This may serve to flatter their intelligence. Many of the more theatrical industries, such as advertising and public relations, are often criticized for their reliance on the "big reveal". They keep everything hush-hush to the point where you would be forgiven for thinking that they were about to reveal the Theory of Relativity. In truth, being magnanimous enough to engage the audience in the thinking before the big day is often hugely beneficial, leading to greater understanding, and much more pertinent questions. (And as you know from the theme of this book, I am a great fan of good questions.) So, consider what their views might be on:

- The facts.
- The control factors that might allow them to dislike your proposal.

- Their feelings.
- Other possible solutions that you might not have looked at.

As the instigator, you need to take a view on whether the attendees would be better off understanding the method in advance. If the people and the culture are well organized, and you think that they will genuinely prepare diligently, then give them the chance to go through how the idea works. It might just increase the likelihood of everybody agreeing with you.

Rules of engagement: what you have to do on the day

- No one can arrive late or leave early.
- No one can leave the room unless there is an emergency (the only two permissible exceptions are a sudden onset of acute diarrhoea or the death of a family member).
- No mobile phones or communication devices of any kind.
- Everyone has to take their watch off and hand it in (this is optional).
- Anyone who is late cannot join in.
- Do not let irrelevant points pollute the agenda.
- Keep the session moving along briskly.
- Intervene to stop arguments.
- Take the mickey out of those who are lazy or fail to contribute energetically.

If you do not have the energy, authority, or mental furniture to do all of this, then admit it straightaway and get someone else to do it.

> *"It is an unfortunate side-effect of the benefit of free speech that people tend to think that, because things may be said, it does not matter if they are."*
>
> **Charles Moore**

Where? Town/city involvement

"Project Wombat is being run out of San Francisco." Fair enough, but you had better be sure how you are going to know what's going on there. The flow of email may or may not help. The fortnightly conference call booked for 5pm may hide a plethora of troubles. Status reports disguise many an evil, and frequently people don't say what they mean. So if you are the city hub for a project, make sure your updates are clear and honest. And if you are on the receiving end of those from another, then insist on the same. If you suspect you are being messed around, or that you aren't getting the full story, then probe deeper. Ask some of the nasty questions in this book. If all else fails, turn up in their office. People find it much harder to lie to your face, and you'll be able to see for yourself whether the stuff they are claiming actually does exist.

Where? Country (multiple centres)

As more and more projects span the world, they often become multi-centred. It was bad enough when we weren't sure if Roger or Stuart were doing it. They were in the same corridor and if it became a bit confusing, we could walk a few paces and sort it out. Now you'll need a conference call at some ungodly hour, a video link with various characters hiding just out of shot, or a regional summit meeting to try to get to the bottom of it. There are so many people, so many nuances of language, and so many cultural differences involved, that you may never find out the truth. Keep pushing for clarity, lest your direction be lost somewhere between Mumbai and Miami.

> *"Sometimes our right hand doesn't know what our far-right hand is doing."*
>
> **Ronald Reagan**

Where? (In)continent

Despite its more frequent scatological use, incontinence actually refers to lack of restraint or control, and this can be a major issue with international projects. Geographical distance between colleagues has the power to enable hundreds of people to do nothing for months on end, all the while claiming it was down to someone else.

> *"'Cover for me'; 'Good idea, boss'; and 'It was like that when I got here'."*
>
> **Homer Simpson's three little sentences to get through life**

Many projects now are transcontinental, taking in Asia, Europe, or the Americas at the touch of a button. Make sure you know who is doing what, where, and why. Otherwise, everyone will claim that it is the responsibility of everyone else.

Where? Worldwide operation

At the supra level, you will often find people these days claiming that something is "worldwide". Treat these types of claims with deep suspicion. There's nothing wrong with multinational cooperation and culturally diverse skills being used on big projects. The knack is getting to straight answers as to who is actually responsible. If they want to wriggle, they'll hide behind time zones, cultural differences, language problems, technology, and a whole host of other clever techniques to prevent you getting to the truth. It all has to happen somewhere, and you have a right to know. So keep being specific, and don't let them be vague.

Wherehousing: dealing with multinational teams

International chaos is a frequent problem, and can be addressed by an approach I call wherehousing. Wherehousing wants to know where the project is housed. It's as simple as that, and yet with many international projects, you would be hard pushed to tell.

> *"We learn from experience that not everything that is incredible is untrue."*
>
> **Cardinal de Reitz**

Take a look at Figure 6.2. I have not made this chart up. It comes from a real multinational organization. All I have done is changed some of the acronyms and substituted my own name for that of the team leader. This chart was generated in response to the question: *"How is your international team organized?"* Simple enough to answer, one might have thought.

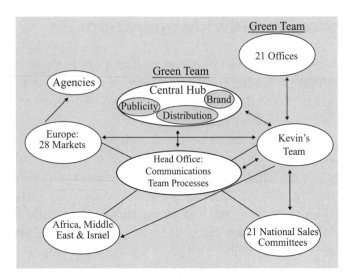

Fig. 6.2: International confusion

Well, clearly, it was not simple. The question might have been, but the answer definitely wasn't. Now it is not my intention to criticize this particular organization, nor the organizational chart that they believe explains how their business works. (As a matter of interest, the word *organagram* does not appear in the dictionary – it seems to have been erroneously invented by businessmen who aspire to being more erudite, but have yet to succeed.) Suffice to say that any normal person would find it impossible to understand who reports to whom in this structure, if indeed it is one.

> *"Democracy is a government by discussion but it is only effective if you can stop people talking."*
>
> **Clement Attlee**

Decreeing the setup of a worldwide project team is similar to herding cats, and may never be adequately resolved, but here are some possible ways of establishing where things should happen. Have a look at Figure 6.3. It all revolves

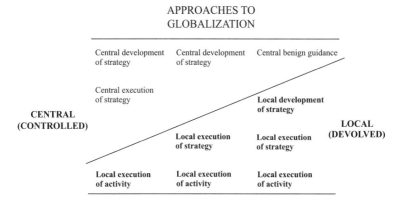

Fig. 6.3: **Approaches to globalization**

around whether decisions and activity are controlled at the centre, or devolved to local markets. And all the shades of grey in between.

To the left of the chart, control at the centre is quite heavy. They won't loosen their grip on the development or execution of the strategy, but they might allow local execution of the activity, such as translation into local language. At the far right, the local people do the lot, with a minimal amount of benign guidance from the centre. This is the closest to a modern version of the "connect and collaborate" model that many companies now favour. No one approach is fundamentally right or wrong, but it really pays you to consider what type of setup you are dealing with, and adjust accordingly. Ask the *Where?* question. Remember wherehousing. If you don't like the answer, try to change it. If you can't, decide whether you can live with it, or, if you can't, move to another company.

Where? feedback

The idea that started in your head may now have circumnavigated the globe. Or it may not have got that far.

Off your desk to a local team and out to a customer may well have been quite far enough. But however far it needs to go, you will at some point be subjected to feedback. This can range from *"This is great, Kevin"* to *"This is utter rubbish and it will never work"*, which basically means: *"Kevin, you are an idiot."* You need to be braced for all extremes, and prepared to hone and refine your thinking based on what you discover. Time lags are irritating too. You may pass several hurdles who reckon your work is excellent, only to have a committee in Hong Kong reject it as culturally inappropriate months later. Refer back to Figure 6.1 and keep going round the loop until you get it right.

The power of context

In his book *The Tipping Point*, Malcolm Gladwell suggests three areas that have a significant bearing on all good communications:

1. *The Law of the Few* – the idea that the nature of the messenger is critical.
2. *The Stickiness Factor* – the quality of the message has to be good enough to be worth acting on.
3. *The Power of Context* – people are exquisitely sensitive to changes of time, place and circumstance.

These should be self-explanatory, but do pay particular attention to the power of context. We talked in the last chapter about timing your run, and the *Where?* element can be just as important to the success of your project. Take care to ask the *Where?* question early enough in the proceedings. Then, if you are not happy with the answer you receive, there is still time to do something about it.

Subsidiary *Where?* questions

A few more thoughts on the *Where?* question. It can lead you off in all sorts of directions, which is fine if you have attended to the main point. Assuming that you have, you may wish to ask:

- Where is the intended market?
- Where to next?
- Where in the world?
- Where is all of this going to happen?
- Where will the result finally exist?

Use these lines of inquiry if you want to consider some of the vagaries that will afflict you in the future.

Wherever

A quick reminder that vagueness won't do. It's a prevailing theme of this book, and just as pertinent to the *Where?* question. If you receive flabby, fuzzy answers, don't stand for it. Keep probing until you get the answers you need.

Wherewithal

The wherewithal is the necessary funds, resources or equipment to get the job done. It may also include the mental furniture, or the expertise at your disposal. Although not strictly a *Where?* question, the word is semantically linked for a reason. You will be left literally no*where* if you haven't got the troops and the skills to handle the job, so take the time to make sure you have.

Wherewolves and how to track them down

Wherewolves is my name for those frightfully modern people who never stay in one place so you never know where they are. Under the approximate guise of remote working, hot desking or some suitable WiFi, WAP-enabled smokescreen, they curiously never seem to turn up anywhere. Don't get me wrong. I'm sure the information revolution has spawned a generation of highly conscientious people doing way more than they ever did before. But that's not true of everyone. There's always someone riding the system, and mobile working is an absolute classic for the shirkers. The Bromley office thinks Barry is at Head Office today. Strangely though, Head Office thinks he's out in the field with the sales force, which he isn't. In truth, bluetoothed up to the gunwales, Barry is having a lie-in, taking the kids to school, and possibly even shacking up in a motel with Shirley from the local pub. So if you can spot a wherewolf in your company, don't put them on your team.

The whereafter

Whereafter is a lovely old word for the bit that happens at the end, or afterwards. It can be a pleasure to reflect on a success, or painful to rake over the bones of a failure. Either way, postmortems are always informative. Look back on your last project and look at where things happened: what can you learn? Once the team has been decided, look carefully at where they are to operate, and where they need to arrive. Scan the ideas in this chapter, and make sure you keep tabs on them. Rest assured, if you don't, they'll probably be up to something that you did not intend.

Summary of *Where?* thinking

1. *Where?* means in, at, or to what place, point, or position?
2. Work out how to get the idea from your head to the outside world.
3. Consider the journey through people, teams, offices and countries.
4. Pay particular attention to worldwide operations and virtual teams.
5. Be aware of the power of context and time your run accordingly.
6. Use wherehousing to specify where multinational teams will work.
7. Whereabouts: consider flexible approaches to globalization.
8. Wherever: do not allow vagueness to creep in.
9. Wherewithal: ensure the necessary funds, resources and equipment.
10. Keep an eye open for wherewolves, and don't choose them for your team.
11. Remember the whereafter: conduct postmortems to learn.

Exercise: Hunt the colleague

1. Write down all the characters you need in order to get the job done. If there are scores of them, just concentrate on the top people whose decisions are crucial, or the ones who are doing all the work, regardless of title.

2. Take a different colour pen, and write down their physical location next to each name. How many different places are listed? How much chaos is there?

3. Take a clean sheet and write the places with the relevant people underneath. Where is the centre of gravity based on the number of relevant bodies in one place? What does that tell you?

4. Which is more important to the project: leadership skills on the spot, or craft skills? If it is the former, then it should probably reside in the same place as the leader. If it is the latter, it may be better placed where the skills are, with the leader keeping an eye on things from elsewhere.

5. Weigh up the pros and cons and choose a central locus for the project.

Do We Really Need to Do This?

This chapter recaps all the questions so far and asks the fail-safe question: Do we really need to do this? *Today, tomorrow, next week, next month, next year, or ever? If it doesn't tick all the boxes, then don't do it. How does this compare with everything else we are doing? Remind yourself: what was the original idea?*

Recap of all the questions so far

If you have got this far, you've done well. Received wisdom has it that few people read beyond the first chapter of a business book. So you've either got superb staying power or you have just dipped into this bit. Either way, read on. We have methodically asked the main fundamental questions that will determine whether your business idea or project is going to work. We have raised the point that an idea that remains just as an idea, and hasn't been enacted, is effectively as useless as not having an idea at all. By this point, you should feel comfortable that you can answer each of the questions that form a chapter heading with a high degree of confidence. So for example:

So what?
You can answer this retort with a clear reason, such as "because it's thoroughly worthwhile and will benefit the business".

Why?
You know precisely why you are doing it.

How?
You have worked out precisely how it can be done, without fudging the answer.

Who?
You have established exactly who will do it, and they have agreed to do so. (Double-check that you have not written

"Action: Emma" on a document somewhere and failed to let her know – this does not count.)

When?
All the timings are sorted out, and deemed to be acceptable by the people who have to deliver them.

Where?
It is crystal clear where the work will be done, and all vague elements of virtual working have been exposed and thrashed out.

It all sounds a bit too good to be true, doesn't it? And it may well be. There are always surprises and nasty developments lurking just around the corner – that's life. If you are convinced that all the answers to these questions are robust and watertight, then there is one final fail-safe that needs to be engaged. It is the question that forms the title of this chapter: *Do we really need to do this?*

The power of *Do we really need to do this?*

Do we really need to do this? cuts to the quick of any business decision. If the decision is a big one, with a lot riding on it, and probably no little investment of time and money, then it will flush out whether everybody involved in the decision is absolutely sure. It provides a last chance to express doubts and check once more that it is the right thing to do to go ahead. If the decision is a small one, then the question has the power to determine whether, on reflection, the proposed activity is a waste of time that won't have any major bearing on the fortunes of the company. If that turns out to be the case, then clearly the proposal should be cancelled or significantly revisited.

> *"Success is the ability to go from one failure to another with no loss of enthusiasm."*
>
> **Winston Churchill**

If it sounds improbable that a proposal might have got this far and still be essentially pointless, I am sad to report that it is not. Thousands of companies every day embark on millions of projects and activities that will never have a positive effect on anything. Whether this (lack of) effect is measured in profit, margin, income, awareness, reputation, morale, or scores of other dimensions, some stuff just doesn't work, and can genuinely be described as a complete waste of time. This is the stuff we are trying to eradicate.

The prevalence of so much pointless and time-wasting activity is, to a degree, testament to the relentless enthusiasm that many humans display as a natural trait. It doesn't apply to everyone, by any means, but many people just want to keep diving in, often flying in the face of previous experience. As Churchill says, we take failure on the chin frequently, and plough on to the "next big thing". The energy in this context is admirable, but the lack of learning in many instances is not. We can do a lot better, more often, simply by paying more attention, and this is what this question is all about.

What *Do we really need to do this?* means

Do we really need to do this? is best deployed when the word *really* is given emphasis. After all the other scrutiny we have given the decision-making process, we are not saying that the idea or project is fundamentally flawed. Not at all. In fact, it is probably on a long list of ideas that probably *could* work. But companies do not have infinite resources or energy, and unless they set simple priorities, then there will be chaos. We can't have everything louder than everything else, and we can't have everything happening first. So it's time to exercise that most treasured of human qualities, free will, and make some decisions about whether this thing really is worth doing.

> "We must believe in free will. We have no choice."
>
> **Isaac Bashevis**

At base level, *Do we really need to do this?* means what it says. But it can mean quite a bit more. It can help to explore whether:

- The team is actually being forced to do something that they don't really agree with.
- On reflection, there isn't actually a clear benefit in any direction.
- Other people want to do it, but you personally don't.

Let's start to look at some possible applications.

How to use the *Do we really need to do this?* question

As usual, it's the facts we are after, not any overblown or biased perspectives that muddy the waters and fool us into believing things, or agreeing to them, when we are just being railroaded by other forces, or lapsing into lazy thinking.

> *"An exaggeration is a truth which has lost its temper."*
>
> **Kahil Gibran**

Stay calm, and evaluate all the parameters as clearly as you can. You can apply your opinion and expertise in due course, but first you want the facts and nothing else. If you attempt to use exaggeration to reinforce your position, you will actually lay yourself open to rejection more easily. Even a fool can spot exaggeration (in fact, many specialize in it). No, analyse the situation forensically like a lawyer or detective, and then use your wiles to win the day. Try some of these questions.

External *Do we really need to do this?* questions

I have divided this question into two levels of emphasis:

1. Do we really *have* to do this?
2. Do we really *need* to do this?

We will deal with each in turn.

Question 1	Subsidiary questions
Do we really *have* to do this?	Are we being ordered to? Who is forcing us? Do we have a choice? If yes, what shall we do? Are there more important things to do?

The emphasis here is on the word "have". Do we really *have* to do this? There are many possible answers, but frequently it just generates more subsidiary questions, like the ones above. So it is important that you don't leave the subsequent set of questions hanging unanswered. You need to chase the absolute answers down to the bitter end, like this.

Subsidiary question	Possible answers
Are we being ordered to?	(a) Yes (b) No (c) Nobody seems to know
Who is forcing us?	(a) Head office (b) The boss in this office (c) No one
Do we have a choice?	(a) Yes (b) No (c) Possibly
If yes, what shall we do?	(a) Agree and get on with it (b) Refuse (c) Argue for something different
Are there more important things to do?	(a) Yes, so let's say so (b) No, this is indeed top priority

Keep going down to the next level if you need to. Here's the second angle of the same question, based on the principle that electing to do something is not the same thing as actually needing to do it.

Question 2	Subsidiary questions
Do we really *need* to do this?	Is it the right answer to the issue? Who exactly will benefit? Who wants it? Is this a need or a want?

Subsidiary question	Possible answer
Is it the right answer to the issue?	(a) Yes, let's proceed (b) No, there are other ways
Who exactly will benefit?	(a) Everyone – it's a great idea (b) Only the project sponsor
Who wants it?	(a) Someone with the company's interests very much at heart (b) Someone who is self-serving and egotistical
Is this a need or a want?	(a) It's a need – we must go ahead (b) It's a want – we could live without it

Keep going as though you were conducting a murder inquiry. Remember: you have to know, otherwise you will only have yourself to blame for being involved in something that isn't getting you or the company anywhere.

Internal *Do we really need to do this*? questions

As with all the other questions, in particularly tough circumstances, you may have to ask the questions internally before going public, or if you haven't been satisfied with the external answers first time round. Try these:

Question	Possible answers
Do I really *have* to do this?	(a) Yes, I have no option (b) No, I could refuse
Do I really *need* to do this?	(a) No. The rest can, but I'm not going to (b) Yes. It will help me and my career

If you are subject to a *fait accompli*, then you will either have to buckle down and get on with it, or refuse to do so and possibly be fired. It's your choice. You'll know what to do, and what the tolerances of your organization are. If the idea is beneficial for the business, but it's not really your bag, then try to find a way of opting out by suggesting someone else with more suitable skills. Just do it as early as you can, and as subtly as possible, citing the best interests of the company, not yourself.

If it doesn't tick all the boxes, don't do it

It's all very well for an author to assert *"If it's like this, do x"*, or *"If it's like that, do y"*, but it's never that cut and dried, is it? You will have to apply your skill and judgement when things are complicated, just as you always do. But there is one basic principle that usually works well in most walks of life:

If it doesn't tick all the boxes, don't do it.

This isn't to say that you are insisting on perfection every time. We are not talking about predicting the end result here, just looking at what you feel about the nature of the work. Draw up a list of criteria that matter to you, and decide whether you are happy with them. They might include:

- Nature of the work
- Reason for the work
- Duration
- Location
- Team members
- Boss

- Proposed method
- Timing
- Your skills
- Repetition: have you done this before?

This list is by no means exhaustive. Write your own. Tick or cross each criterion based on your degree of happiness with it. If the list is long (up to 10 items), you may tolerate a couple of crosses. If it is short, you should only be satisfied if they are all ticked.

Do we really need to do this? Today

Extra poignancy can be added to *Do we really need to do this*? by adding a proposed timing, such as today, tomorrow, or any point in the future. As a rough rule of thumb, the quicker something can be done, the less complicated it is. The less complicated it is, the less important it may well be, but not necessarily. The time element does however bring into sharp relief the necessity of doing something. Let's say it has been agreed that Project Jelly Mould is an excellent idea. Then imagine all assembled saying: *"Great. Let's start today."* If today seems inappropriate, but tomorrow seems okay, this tells you something about Project Jelly Mould. If starting next week seems laughable, then how serious is everybody about it? Try asking the question and then filling in the suggested moment of starting.

- Do we really need to do this? Today
- Do we really need to do this? Tomorrow
- Do we really need to do this? Next week
- Do we really need to do this? Next month
- Do we really need to do this? Next year
- Do we really need to do this? Ever

> *"It is always better to have no ideas than false ones; to believe nothing than to believe what is wrong."*
>
> **Thomas Jefferson**

If there is no particular reason to start today, then look for simple reasons. If it's too soon, then fair enough. If people need preparation time, then ditto. If everybody is unusually busy today, but they won't be tomorrow, then that's okay.

Do we really need to do this? Tomorrow

Everything has to start sometime, and tomorrow is as good a time as any. Let's do it tomorrow. If you suggest tomorrow and receive a lukewarm response, then ask yourself why. The usual platitudes about being too busy, clearing the diary, and work commitments will be bandied about, but what are the true underlying reasons?

> *"All great ideas are logical in hindsight."*
>
> **Frank Whittle**

Starting something is the engine that creates forward motion. Without the start, there is no middle or end, and so no Project Jelly Mould. So fast forward in your mind to the end, and work out how soon it should start.

Do we really need to do this? Next week

"Robert is on holiday this week, so we'll start week commencing the third." Is he really? And why exactly can

we not start without him? Do not fall victim to the "not-quite-complete team" syndrome. It's a very rare thing if everyone on a project is ever present at the same time anyway. Take an example of six team members. Each has four weeks' holiday a year. That's 24 weeks to interlock, and there will be a decree somewhere that says that no one can go away at the same time, although the rule will doubtless be flaunted.

> *"How many pessimists end up by desiring the things they fear, in order to prove they are right?"*
>
> **Robert Mallet**

Now add in an allowance for illness, emergency family days, travel, and the all-pervasive awayday. You'll probably find that crucial team members are out of the equation for months on end. So next week might be as good as any.

Do we really need to do this?
Next month

Ah yes, seasonal variations. Chapter 5 dealt with the time issue in detail, but for now let's just strip it down to the sort of stuff that people say about the months of the year. You know the sort of thing:

January is no good because people are still returning from Christmas.
February is thin because loads of people go skiing at half term with the family.
March is a possible, assuming we have got our act together this year (see January/February).
April is no good because of Easter.

May is riddled with Bank Holidays, so everything is disjointed.

June usually has the World Cup or some other massive sporting distraction.

July is a heat wave, so everyone is drinking lager in the sun.

August is hopeless because the whole of continental Europe is shut.

September catches people on the hop because they are all still returning from their holidays, and everyone is behind.

October is another half term holiday write-off.

November is a possible, but there are always lots of absences through flu.

December is useless because everyone is in the pub with a silly hat on.

(*Return to January in a desperate attempt to boost productivity.*)

Looking at this set of truisms, it's a miracle that anything ever gets done at all, isn't it? Just beware of people who say they'll start next month. There will always be another excuse.

Do we really need to do this?
Next year

Now we really are drifting off into the mists of time. Who says you will be here next year anyway? Who says the company will be? Companies need to realize that their track record in this department is poor. Expecting employees to pledge to a gargantuan effort in a year's time flies in the face of the hundreds of stories of people being "surplus to requirements" suddenly on a cold Friday in December. No, let's keep the start point somewhere very much in range.

Do we really need to do this? Ever

As Graham Edmonds says in his book *Liar's Paradise*, there are seven degrees of corporate deceit.

1. **White lie:** told to make someone feel better or to avoid embarrassment.
2. **Fib:** relatively insignificant, such as excuses and exaggerations.
3. **Blatant:** whoppers used when covering up mistakes or apportioning blame.
4. **Bullshit:** a mixture of those above combined with spin and bluff to give the best impression.
5. **Political:** similar to bullshit but with much bigger scale and profile.
6. **Criminal:** illegal acts from fraud to murder, and their subsequent denial.
7. **Ultimate:** so large that it must be true. As Joseph Goebbels said: "If you tell a lie big enough and keep repeating it, people will eventually come to believe it."

There is a summary of the book in the Appendix.

> *"Never admit a lie – simply keep repeating it."*
>
> **Joseph Goebbels**

Sad to report, sometimes the answer to the question *Do we really need to do this?* might actually be: no, never. We desperately hope that this is not the case, given all the other investigative work you have been through, but it's possible. Everybody may have been subject to anything from a level-one to a level-four lie. Companies, teams, and individuals, particularly those in positions of power, are eminently capable of convincing themselves that something is hugely important, when it patently isn't. You only have to look at politics to understand that this is true, even though it is a bit shocking.

How does this compare with everything else we are doing?

Another way to pressure test whether something is genuinely worth doing is to compare it with the importance of something else, or everything else. Have a look at how Project Jelly Mould compares with all the other things that you or the company are doing, and see how it stacks up. If it is found wanting, think again.

> *"Nothing is more dangerous than an idea when it is the only one you have."*
>
> **Emile Chartier**

If you are having difficulty in comparing one thing with another, try using a comparative framework. There are scores to choose from and, if you can, use one that is particular to your industry or the nature of the project. If you don't have anything suitable, try these two techniques from my previous books.

The Priority Matrix (Figure 7.1) helps you to work out what is more important than something else. If it is urgent and important, do it now. If it is urgent but not important, delegate it, or get it out of the way first. If it is important but not urgent, think about what you need to do and plan ahead. If it is neither important nor urgent, ditch it.

THE PRIORITY MATRIX

URGENT

DELEGATE OR DO FIRST, QUICKLY	DO NOW
IGNORE OR CANCEL	THINK AND PLAN

NOT IMPORTANT — IMPORTANT

NOT URGENT

Fig. 7.1:   Priority Matrix

The Growing Pane (Figure 7.2) helps you to sort out good and bad working practices. Good, old practices should have their relevance confirmed and be kept. Good, new ones should be used to inspire more. New, bad practices need to

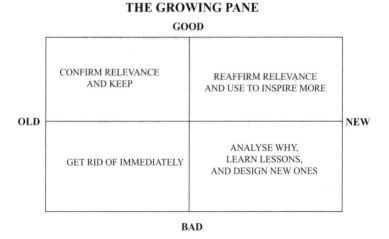

THE GROWING PANE

GOOD

CONFIRM RELEVANCE AND KEEP	REAFFIRM RELEVANCE AND USE TO INSPIRE MORE
GET RID OF IMMEDIATELY	ANALYSE WHY, LEARN LESSONS, AND DESIGN NEW ONES

OLD — NEW

BAD

Fig. 7.2:   Growing Pane

be analysed to find out why they are bad, and replaced by new ones. Get rid of the old, bad ones immediately.

What's the point of this?

If an issue really needs unclogging, but no one is coming to the point and sorting it out, then you may need to be blunt. If you decide not to, that's your choice, but don't blame anyone else if you end up months later enacting something that is nuts when you didn't have the balls to point out the defects in the first place.

What's the point of this? is highly direct but it needn't be rude. Use it as a last resort if you really can't see the point of what you are being asked to do.

> *"The great enemy of clear language is insincerity."*
>
> **George Orwell**

To what effect?

The *What?* question receives a quick review in Chapter 10, but its cousin *To what effect?* can be highly effective in its own right. If you have been bombarded with flabby answers such as *"Because Graham says so"*, try pushing for a more robust one that actually attempts to explain the effect of what is being proposed. This usually exposes those projects that are essentially pointless.

> *"It is hard to believe a man is telling the truth when you know that you would lie if you were in his place."*
>
> **H. L. Mencken**

Remind me. What *was* the original idea?

For those who have veered massively off the main point, this hits them right between the eyes. Try it.

"Remind me. What was *the original idea?"*

Half the time the person who is twittering on about objectives, timelines and data capture can't actually remember what the original idea was. This question is one of the most powerful in your *So what?* arsenal, particularly if there has been a long time lag between the original proposal and the moment when it is all drifting horribly off course. Remember, you are not being perverse or unpleasantly subversive – you are just asking for the truth.

> *"The easiest thing in the world is to tell the truth. Then you don't have to remember what you said."*
>
> **Robert Evans**

Do we really need to do this? summary

1. Recap all the questions so far.
2. Ask *Do we really need to do this?*
3. Ask externally first, then internally if you need a rethink.
4. If it doesn't tick all the boxes, don't do it.
5. Consider the Today/Tomorrow/Next week/Month/Year/Ever answers.
6. How does this compare with everything else we are doing?

7. Ask *What's the point of this?*
8. Ask *To what effect?*
9. Ask a colleague: *Remind me. What* was *the original idea?*

Exercise: Ever or never

1. Remind yourself of all the questions you have posed on your quizzical journey. Are you happy with the quality and robustness of the answers you have received? These may have come from you or from colleagues.

2. Jot down on one sheet of paper the justification for the project or activity that is proposed. Now apply the sense-check: *Do we really need to do this?*

3. Ask the question of yourself first, several times. If you are satisfied, then proceed. If you are not, then go and ask the same question of a colleague whose opinion you really respect (there's no point in asking an idiot!).

4. If you receive sensible reasons and are now satisfied, then proceed. If you do not, then consider your options for removing yourself from the project or using what power you have to stop it from happening.

5. If you choose to stop it altogether, bear in mind that everyone has come a long way, so they won't like your stance. Spend some time mustering powerful arguments and considering how to break it to them gently.

Something Must be Wrong if...?

This chapter covers the power of completing the sentence "Something must be wrong if…" *Be wary of multiple excuses: no one wants to do it, everyone claims to be too busy, there are other more pressing matters, postponement is suggested, lack of budget or resources. Grapple with internal worries such as: I don't fancy it, I've got a horrible feeling it's all going to go wrong, and I never did like the idea anyway. Pay attention to the little voices: the power of honesty and the value of speaking up.*

The power of *Something must be wrong if...*

There is a completely different way to find out if something is worth doing or not. In the last chapter, we approached it by using the open-ended question *Do we really need to do this?* This, of course, allows the persuasive or quick-witted respondent to make it sound as though there is indeed an excellent reason to proceed, thereby leaving you floundering in the corridor wishing you had never asked. If the answer was robust and included something you hadn't considered, then there may well be a case for retiring gracefully to lick your wounds and consider whether you are just a born cynic.

> *"It is an intelligent man who knows when he has lost an argument."*
>
> **Alistair Maclean**

But I don't want to believe that you are a cynic who can't see the benefit of anything – just a naturally inquisitive person who doesn't want to embark on something pointless when the reasons for it haven't been made clear to you. Assuming that this is indeed the case, then it may help to try completing the sentence *Something must be wrong if...* Unlike the open-ended question, this forces you, or any colleague in whom you confide, to fill in the rest of the sentence. The only way to do this is to draw on your natural knowledge of the situation, or, if you are not sure, to go and look for more information or reasons.

What *Something must be wrong if...* means

What the completed sentence does is to highlight what is already wrong, or what may well go wrong. It is not a mantra for pessimists. It is more a rallying call for realists. Realists know that, in all probability, something will go wrong. It always does. This does not mean that they are gloomy all the time, nor that they refuse to do anything that isn't perfect. No, it's not that at all. They just tend to be a bit more mature, often more experienced, and they don't expect a perfect ride. Ever.

> *"If you don't learn to laugh at trouble, you won't have anything to laugh at when you're old."*
>
> **Edgar Watson Howe**

Riding the rollercoaster of a project at work is either a source of massive stress or regular amusement. You just have to choose which attitude you would like to adopt. You will live longer if you laugh at trouble, tweak the nose of chaos, and generally wave your privates at all those little disasters that happen on the way. Part of the knack of having this more relaxed attitude to life is always to be on the lookout for the stuff that, in all probability, will go wrong. Then it won't be such a meltdown when it actually does. One of the great surprises about people who are constantly surprised in business is that they are surprised. That's a lot of surprises, I'll admit, and that's the very point. If they took five minutes a week to work out all the things that will probably go wrong, then they wouldn't be surprises, now would they? Completing the sentence would help them hugely, and it can certainly help you.

How to use the *Something must be wrong if...* statement

You should use it to thrash out what is already wrong with a proposal, idea or project. Or what *might* be wrong with it. Or what probably *will* go wrong. Any of these may be valid reasons to pull out or rethink. If it's wrong *already*, then you should have severe reservations and may need to take drastic action. If you think it *might* go wrong, you need to pressure test your hunch and try to articulate why – first to yourself, and then to a colleague to make sure you are not going mad. If you think it definitely will go wrong, then you need as close as you can get to proof. It's no use steaming in to the project leader and telling them it's rubbish because something unspecified may or may not happen at some point in the distant future. They will have a sense of humour failure for sure, and you'll look daft.

> *"The one thing I have learned over the years is the difference between taking one's work seriously and one's self seriously. The first is imperative and the second is disastrous."*
>
> **Margot Fonteyn**

For more on this, do look at *Teach Yourself Running Your Business*, p. 84 (*Take the issues seriously, but not yourself*). Meanwhile, muster the evidence you need and fill in the second part of some of these statements.

External *Something must be wrong if...* statements

The distinction between external and internal statements needs a quick explanation in the context of this statement. The external versions do not necessarily require you to ask questions of your colleagues. So long as they have made their opposition clear, then you can effectively fill in the second half of the sentence on their behalf. If you are unaware of their position, then clearly you can't, but by now you should be. The internal versions are for your thought processes only, and are more to do with the dark demons gnawing away at your conscience. We'll look at those in a minute. For now, let's see if there is anything wrong with the team, or the subject matter of the proposed project. I can't predict what the second half of your sentence(s) will be, but here are some possibilities.

Something must be wrong if...	no one wants to do it.
	everyone claims to be too busy.
	there are other more pressing matters, apparently.
	postponement is suggested.
	there isn't enough budget.
	the right resources aren't immediately available.

If you come up with one massive problem straightaway, then consider whether it is a deal breaker or not. Is it so enormous that it can't be solved, thereby rendering the project pointless? If so, talk to someone immediately. If it's just a small thing, work out how to solve it without boring anyone else. If it's lots of small things, then take a little longer to do exactly the same thing. For a full rundown on how to do this, have a look at the exercise at the end of this chapter. Now let's have a look at what completing the sentence might have thrown up.

No one wants to do it

Oops. That's a bit of a giveaway, isn't it? If no one else does, then why should you? Is the whole thing a massive banana skin or a booby trap? You should be deeply suspicious of any proposal that no one else wants to touch. The subject matter may be grim. There may be those who know things that you don't. The idea may be culturally incompatible with what the company is all about. Newcomers initiate these types of projects all the time, and they rarely see the light of day. Anyway, don't get paranoid. Just make sure that you know exactly what's going on, and why.

Everyone claims to be too busy

Yeah, right! You, of course, have absolutely nothing to do! Buck passing is an art, and there are always plenty of people in companies who are brilliant at it. You should not aspire to being good at it, nor should you be the passive recipient of all sorts of stuff that, frankly, should be done by someone else. If everyone else says they are frantically busy, then maybe the project isn't so crucial after all.

There are other more pressing matters, apparently

Ah, there's the rub. If it is a simple matter to nominate all sorts of other activities and projects that are obviously more important than the proposal on the table, then it doesn't take a genius to rumble that it cannot be deemed high priority. And if it's not high priority, then it's not immediately necessary. And if it's not immediately necessary, then... well, you get the idea. Try to apportion a degree of importance to the matter in hand, and if you find it wanting, be suspicious of it and investigate further. The "facts" are often not quite what they seem to be.

> *"Get your facts first, and then you can distort them as much as you please."*
>
> **Mark Twain**

Postponement is suggested

If a project or activity is postponed or delayed, there may be something fishy going on. Don't get me wrong. I am not naturally suspicious, and the degree to which you take something as gospel may well be related to the integrity of the person who told you. But I do propose that you pursue your lines of inquiry so that you do get the full story. Then you can make proper decisions. As a general rule, rock solid ideas don't get postponed. If anything, they get fast tracked, brought forward, or rushed out to catch a market opportunity. So if someone suggests that Project Lamp Stand is *"delayed until Quarter 4"*, then you should question whether it is worth working on it at all.

Filling in the rest of the sentence will help focus the mind considerably.

There isn't enough budget

This is a dead giveaway. Management are apparently "deeply committed" to Project Lamp Stand and yet, strangely, Geoff doesn't seem to have a budget for it. What it basically means is that the management know that they should be putting resources behind such an idea, but they are not. Good management puts their money where their mouth is immediately. Bad management is too spineless, can't see the wood for the trees, doesn't want the responsibility, is slow, lazy, or too dim to spot the true potential of the opportunity. So if there is no budget, or very little, look for deeper explanations. The project may well be a dead duck already, so don't waste your time.

The right resources aren't immediately available

This is another fudge. Either the A team is going to be put on the job, or they are not. Time is either of the essence, or an irrelevance. So for full evidence of the import of any given initiative, you want to see the best people on the case straightaway. If it doesn't happen, then the powers that be are not fully behind it, so you could be wasting your time, again. If this becomes apparent, you may need to point it out, although you might not be that popular when you do.

> *"Criticism is prejudice made plausible."*
>
> **H. L. Mencken**

Internal *Something must be wrong if...* statements

Let's assume that, publicly, there are plausible answers to most of the above questions. But you still have your doubts. It's time to try the same exercise, but this time to direct the power of the sentence at yourself. Write down all your possible completed sentences. They may be something like this:

Something must be wrong if...

I don't fancy it.
I've got a horrible feeling it's all going to go wrong.
I never did like the idea anyway.
I don't like the people I'm working with.
I don't want to go to work in the morning.
I can't be bothered to fill in the rest of this sentence.

I don't fancy it

What's the matter with you? If you don't fancy it, you need to articulate as dispassionately as you can what the reasons are. If you think the project is fundamentally flawed or misguided, then you may have a valid point. It is late in the day though, so you really should have had time by now to air your reservations. If there is any reason linked to an undesirable character trait (on your behalf), such as laziness or politics, then I am afraid that doesn't count as a valid reason. It's a bit like having a sick note at school – you need to be genuinely ill to get off lessons. If you are political or lazy, then no one will be impressed with your opinion anyway. If you just don't fancy it, but you can't explain why sensibly, then it's your problem. Think of something more substantial.

I've got a horrible feeling it's all going to go wrong

This may well be valid, depending on the context. If you are a permanent pessimist, then I'm afraid that's not a good enough reason. On the other hand, if you are massively experienced at this type of work, and you can see pitfalls in the idea, timing plan, methodology, or any other element of it, then it is your responsibility to highlight what that is. There are plenty of instances when charismatic leaders have persuaded huge gangs of people to do mad things. You only have to look at some despotic world leaders to acknowledge that, and it happens in companies all the time.

> *"Those who can make you believe absurdities can make you commit atrocities."*
>
> **Voltaire**

So if you believe this is what's happening on a particular project, you need to think carefully about how you raise it. In the old fable, it was the child who pointed out that the king wasn't actually wearing any clothes at all, and that may well be your role here. Tread carefully though – there will be lots of other characters around with a vested interest in the thing going ahead regardless of how nuts it is.

I never did like the idea anyway

Er, no, I am afraid this is not a valid reason. This is the last refuge of the spineless detractor, and it just won't wash. If you have genuinely got yourself into a position where a project is thoroughly well justified, you are slated to be part of it, and now you don't want to, then you only have yourself to blame. You see, it was your duty to point this out at the very beginning, which you have patently failed to do. The good news, however, is that if you are reading this whilst you are at the inception of a project that you don't think is a good idea, then it might nudge you to do something about it right now.

I don't like the people I'm working with

A tricky one, this. It is perfectly possible that you are surrounded by weirdos, bullies and dimwits, but if that really is the case, then are you in the right company? Most people are essentially well meaning, and most operate within a reasonable range of competence. Try to whittle this feeling down to its constituent parts. Is it the whole gang you can't stand? Or is it just one person, perhaps a very powerful or highly influential individual? It's a significant difference. If you conclude that you really don't like all of them, then you should either resign, or have a good look at yourself. Are you are a curmudgeon or a grumpy moaner yourself? Is it you, not them, that's the problem here? Be as honest as you can. The least confrontational route is to quietly withdraw yourself from the project base whilst citing the presence of more appropriate skills elsewhere in the company.

I don't want to go to work in the morning

Now this is getting quite serious. *Something must be wrong if...* has a knack of flushing out bigger issues than just the immediate task being considered. Is there a larger malaise at play here? If you don't fancy the idea, if you think everything is going to go wrong and it fills you with dread, if you can't get along with your colleagues, and you don't even fancy going to work in the morning, then you've got some severe problems. I sincerely hope that you don't feel this way. A common trait of those who are really struggling is that they pile one problem on top of another until they cannot see a way out at all. Sane, rational people approach problems by thinking them through one by one, and fixing each one at a time. If you feel you can't cope, get help straightaway.

I can't be bothered to fill in the rest of this sentence

Well, that's the end of the line then, isn't it? Apathy has the power to paralyse any individual, and if it spreads, then it will take the company down too. That's not what we want. If you are suffering from a sustained motivation crisis, you need to work hard to shake yourself out of it. Reasonably high energy levels, a positive attitude and a healthy dose of enthusiasm are what make you a pleasure to be with, and a success at work. Whatever you decide, do not wallow in your own misery and make matters worse.

> *"It is astonishing what foolish things one can temporarily believe if one thinks too long alone."*
>
> **Keynes**

Little voices: the value of speaking up

All the reservations in this chapter are better off aired and sorted out. If your head is full of little voices saying that this is nuts, then you need to reaffirm your concerns, and then go public. Speaking up is always good news. That's how the company gets the benefit of your opinion. Those who say nothing contribute nothing. If you keep your head down and only metaphorically "wear the company uniform", you'll never go anywhere interesting. Don't passively go along with the prevailing view. On many occasions, the majority are wrong. It should be your challenge, and pleasure, to speak up, and swim in the opposite direction if necessary.

> *"One of the delights known to age, and beyond the grasp of youth, is that of Not Going."*
>
> **J. B. Priestley**

The power of honesty

Speaking up has to involve honesty. The old phrase about being "economical with the truth" hides a darker characteristic. We live in such an age of spin that it seems that in many contexts we have lost the simple ability to distinguish between lies and the truth. If you believe something strongly, but don't actually say it, then that is as good as having no opinion. More fundamentally, if you know something that they don't, and you refuse to say it, then you are getting quite close to lying.

> *"Men hate those to whom they have to lie."*
>
> **Victor Hugo**

This is particularly important if what you *haven't* said has a direct bearing on the success or failure of the project. Not speaking up could jeopardize the whole thing, possibly putting jobs at risk. So don't worry about upsetting people – it's better to come out with it and tell the truth than to disguise something important.

> *"When ideas fail, words come in very handy."*
>
> **Goethe**

That's not a licence to come out with stuff when actually you don't have a firm view or a solid idea of how to improve things. Any fool can sit in the wings criticizing everything whilst simultaneously offering no suggestions as to how to make things better. Don't let this be you. Nobody likes negative moaners – they serve no helpful purpose in life, let alone in business.

Something must be wrong if... summary

1. The *Something must be wrong if...* statement is a powerful counterpoint to open-ended questions.
2. Fill in the rest of the sentence to reveal the nasty element that hasn't been raised yet.
3. Establish the prevailing view, or work out if no one is speaking up about it.
4. Look carefully for excuses such as no one wants to do it, everyone claims to be too busy, suggested postponement, or lack of budget and resources.
5. Use internal *Something must be wrong if...* statements to reveal your own reservations.
6. These may include: I don't fancy it, I've got a horrible feeling it's all going to go wrong, I never did like the idea anyway, or I don't like the people I'm working with.
7. If it's so bad that you don't want to go to work in the morning, then get help.
8. If little voices are telling you important things, then speak up and be honest.

> *"Comment is free but facts come on expenses."*
>
> **Tom Stoppard**

Exercise: Fill in the rest of this sentence

1. Start with the sentence *Something must be wrong if...* Write it down on a bit of paper leaving enough space for you to fill in the rest of the sentence.

2. If, after a short while, you can't think of anything, then that's really good news. It means that everything is essentially okay, and that the sense-check has performed its function. You can now proceed with the project, confident in the knowledge that it should essentially be fine.

3. If the first thing you fill in is really significant and nasty, dwell on it for a while and work out what you are going to do. Then try filling in some more to see if there are actually lots of large problems. If so, then that adds additional weight to your case when you go and raise it with someone.

4. If the only thing that emerges is something relatively trivial, then don't hold it up as a reason not to proceed. Spend some constructive time working out how to solve the problem. Once you have, then decide whether you need to explain that to someone, or whether you will simply wait until it crops up, and then offer the solution.

5. If you come up with quite a few trivial things, then just take a little longer to work out how to solve them. They remain trivial, and just because there are more of them doesn't give them greater weight. If necessary, allocate a bit of extra time to solving them all before moaning to your colleagues or gloomily predicting that the project is a non-starter.

Are We There Yet?

This chapter covers learning from children, surviving long journeys and the power of the question: Are we there yet? *Dealing with problems. The value of originality. The power of synectics. How to question everything like a child. A final round up of questions. Are you ready to make the leap?*

Learning from children

The inspiration for the title of this chapter comes from my daughter Shaunagh. *Are we there yet?* is the classic cry from the back of the car when children are getting bored on a long journey. Kids have almost no sense of distance, unless they can stand and point at the destination from where they are, but that's never going to be a long journey. So if you say you are off to visit Grandma, they have no framework on which to base the nature of the journey. Is it 500 yards or 500 miles? They don't know, they don't need to know, and they probably don't even want to know. All they care about is arriving, because that's when the fun starts. I'm not suggesting for one moment that a trip to see Grandma is the high point of a child's week, but at least they know there will be something to investigate at the end, even if it's the corner of the room after injudiciously breaking a window.

As well as being absolutely true of very young children (say, under 10 years old), it remains the case in many instances even into their teens, usually until they have to drive somewhere themselves. Teenagers are eminently capable of having a great weekend on the coast, without knowing what town they were in, or how they got there. Any parent who despairs and says they should concentrate more is missing the point. And that is very much the sentiment behind this book: as grown-ups, we have lost our childlike lines of inquiry, and we are the worse off for it. Kids don't care about the bit in the middle because they are concentrating on the stuff at the end, which is a darn sight more fun and interesting.

Surviving long journeys

My mother is from Land's End and my father was from John o'Groats. Apart from going some way to explaining my contradictory nature, this made visiting the grandparents in the sixties something of a challenge. Every summer I would be secreted into the back of a Ford Consul (white paintwork, red leather seats) and transported on a round trip of 700 miles to Scotland and Cornwall. The extent of the expedition rendered the *Are we there yet?* question somewhat pointless. As far as a six-year-old boy was concerned, you were never there, for days on end.

The joy of arriving thus needed replacing with the art of expectation. As any mature traveller will tell you, the journey is the whole point. Many will say that it is better to travel than to arrive – a pretty controversial assertion for many, one would have thought. The observation is well made, though, because life is not about a series of fixed points at which we magically arrive. It takes effort, time, and sometimes a lot of upsets to "arrive" where we wish. It's the same for companies. Viewed another way, how many "arrivals" would you expect to achieve per year? By which I mean, the very point at which you have achieved something that you have been striving for? I would expect the answer to be in single figures. Given that there are 365 days in a year, that's a pretty low strike rate. So you might as well adjust your thinking to enjoy all the bits in between, because there are a lot more of them than there are arrival points.

The power of *Are we there yet?*

Are we there yet? can help you to pinpoint and articulate a really good sense of perspective on the pace and progress of any project. Understanding time is a crucial component of being successful in business. It also helps reduce your frustration levels in other aspects of your life. Everyone views time differently, and we considered some of these differences in Chapter 5. Corporate time moves slower than normal time, and this can be massively frustrating for people who just want to get on with it. Time lags in projects are almost standard practice. It would be fascinating to see a statistic of the number of projects that actually occur on time. Of course, no such statistic exists, but if it did, I would hazard a guess that at least 80% of them are delayed in some way.

Are we there yet? enables you to get a quick reading on the status of something. In World War II, bomber pilots would call back to their rear gunners for a "stat rep" after an attack. The standard reply that they developed was SNAFU: Situation Normal, All F**ked Up. Enough said. Nothing is ever perfect. Confusion or chaos was regarded as the normal state in war, and it remains that way in many businesses. There's no harm in pointing it out. In fact, it helps your sense of humour. If anyone in authority gets grumpy about it, then it just proves that they have a warped, idealized view of how the world works (or fails to work). Needless to say, such people need to be challenged regularly, and this book is designed to equip you to do it.

> *"If you attack the establishment long and hard enough they will make you a member of it."*
>
> **Art Buchwald**

How to use the *Are we there yet?* question

The *Are we there yet?* question should be used to get to grips with the temporal and completion elements of any project. Earlier questions have established other parameters. *Why?* provides the raison d'être for the activity. *How?* outlines the methodology. *Who?* defines the personnel. *Where?* determines the geography.

When? provides the temporal platform for the three main components of *Are we there yet?.* Namely:

1. Where are we?
2. Where *should* we be by now?
3. Have we arrived at the end point?

Viewed as a straight time line from beginning to end, this question should flush out whether the project is:

1. On time.
2. Late.
3. Finished.

External *Are we there yet?* questions

So let's delve into the question and its possible answers. On first asking, *Are we there yet?* will almost always yield another question in response: *Where is there?* There is no point in trying to answer it accurately if no one can agree on where *there* is. Although this sounds a bit daft, we all know very well that getting clear definitions in business can be a nightmare, so actually it is perfectly possible that loads of people genuinely do not know where *there* is. Let's establish that first.

Original question	Subsidiary question
Are we there yet?	Where is *there*?

Subsidiary question	Possible answers
Where is *there*?	(a) The beginning (b) The end (c) A precise point in the plan that we can clearly define, recognize, and agree on

In most cases, the answer will not be (a) or (b). The reason for this is that very few people ask *Are we there yet?* at the beginning of something, and if you have reached the end, someone will be crowing about it so you will most likely know already. It's the massive bit in the middle, the line that takes up 99% of the project, that causes all the trouble. You'll recall that in Chapter 5 we called this extended wasteland the liveline.

So we want to know where we have reached so far (based on a sensible definition that we all understand) and if we are going to arrive on time. This could get way too hypothetical for a book to cover, so I am going to assume that you and your colleagues have got the mental furniture and maturity to agree on a clear statement of where *there* is. So now we can look at other possible answers to the main question.

Original question	Possible answers
Are we there yet?	(a) We are on time (b) We are late (c) We are finished

These possible answers lead to subsequent possible courses of action. Consider where you are in the grand scheme of things.

Answer	Possible courses of action
We are on time	(a) Great. Say nothing. Everyone will be delighted when we arrive on schedule for once.
	(b) Tell everyone straightaway. Morale is low and we could do with some good news.
	(c) Look harder. What could yet go wrong?
We are late	(a) Fair enough. We can live with it.
	(b) It's a disaster and it can't be put right. We need to tell the relevant people right now.
	(c) It can't be put right but judiciously warning people this far in advance will manage their expectations appropriately.
	(d) Close examination of the rest of the schedule shows that we can catch up time elsewhere, thereby remaining on time.
We are finished	(a) Great. Tell everyone and revel in the moment of arrival.
	(b) Pause for a second. Is there any other refinement we can make to improve it, assuming there is a little slack?
	(c) Okay. What shall we do next?

Internal *Are we there yet?* questions

As is so often the case, there may be a significant discrepancy between the external view of what the state of affairs is, and your personal, internal opinion. In other words, their answer to the *Are we there yet?* question is not the same as yours. If that's the case, then try these.

Prevailing point of view (external claim)	My point of view (internal claim)
We are on time	(a) That's what they are claiming, but I don't believe it.
	(b) Their definition of "on time" isn't the same as mine.

	(c) They are stretching the truth. I can see that it is on the verge of going wrong but they are not admitting it.
We are late	(a) I agree, but they are not prepared to do anything about it.
	(b) We are, and all they've done is delay the end point, which isn't good enough.
We are finished	(a) No we're not, we have cut corners.
	(b) There are more surprises about to emerge that will set us back.

If you have opinions of this type that conflict with those of your colleagues, you need to deal with the problem(s).

Dealing with problems

Figure 9.1 shows a hypothetical state of affairs involving a conflict between you and a colleague. The line between "you" and "me" represents the potential channel of communication. This may well be the phone, email, or a video conference, but preferably it will be conducted in

DEALING WITH PROBLEMS

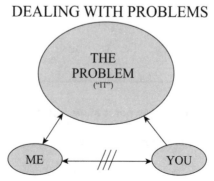

Fig. 9.1: **Dealing with problems**

person. These other methods are not very well suited to the tricky business of grappling with a disagreement.

If you are able to resolve your problem by calm, direct debate, then that's precisely what you should do. More often than not though, things get heated and tempers flare. Things can get personal, and that doesn't help anybody.

The hashed line crossing the line between "you" and "me" is there to indicate that you should not go hell for leather to criticize the individual who represents the other side of what you believe to be right or wrong. As a mature grown-up, your job is to depersonalize the issue and offer a palatable way through that both sides can agree on.

One helpful way to do this is to describe the problem as "it". By doing this, you immediately change the language from confrontational to constructive, thereby hugely increasing your chances of reaching a decent resolution.

Have a look at the linguistic differences between these phrases.

Assertion	Nature of comment
You have screwed this up	Personal insult
Your department has screwed this up	Professional insult
This is a tricky problem, isn't it?	True but fair

No self-respecting colleague will let you get away with the first two. They will dig in, and probably insult you or your department back. There will be pointless deadlock, and a lot of hurt pride. The third one, however, cleverly deploys the "it" word to depersonalize the issue. This allows both parties to retain their dignity, and increase the chances of a positive outcome.

> *"If you are swimming to the shore, it matters little whether you drown in the water or die on the beach."*
>
> **Cheerful Spanish metaphor**

Assertion	Constructive platform
This is a tricky problem, isn't it?	(a) I suggest we resolve it by doing x. (b) I suggest x. What do you suggest? (c) Is there anyone else who could help?

The value of originality

The *Are we there yet?* question values answers that contain original thinking. As soon as the response comes back as "no", clever ideas may well be needed to push things along closer to a "yes". Intrinsically bright people frequently have great ideas all of their own accord, but most of us need a bit of help. Random calling of brainstorm meetings with all the wrong personnel won't help, but there is an approach that might.

The power of synectics

One springboard for creativity that can be useful for generating more original ideas is synectics. The word essentially means working together from outside.

Synectics: a method of identifying and solving problems that depends on creative thinking, the use of analogy, and informal conversation among a small group of individuals with diverse experience and expertise

The rough idea is to remove yourself from the current state of affairs and think laterally about the problem. If you find this hard to do, then engage the services of someone who really doesn't know anything about it. That way, their thinking and suggestions cannot be polluted by anything that might lead to unoriginal thinking. Using analogy as a lever, and likening the circumstances to analogous ones in other categories and markets, can often unclog your current thinking. For a range of suggestions and exercises to help this process, have a look at *Flicking Your Creative Switch* by Wayne Lotherington (there is a summary in the Appendix).

The overall lesson is to regard informal conversation from unlikely sources as being equally valuable to problem solving as the opinions of experts, who can often get bogged down in paralysing detail.

Other childish questions

It also pays great dividends to imagine that you are a child once more. Have a think about all the sorts of questions a child would ask about the subject matter.

You know the sort of thing:

- What's that?
- Why is it blue?
- Why is it that long?

- Why does it go like that?
- Yes, but why?

If you think children are irritating in their pursuit of the clear truth, then just think how much trouble you have answering this supposedly very simple question.

What do you do at work, daddy?
Or mummy, of course. Unless you can point to something clear, such as a fireman or a doctor, chances are you will descend into some meaningless drivel about sales, administration, and, doubtless, pushing boundaries in some revolutionary direction. You could forgive your son or daughter for replying: *So what?*

> *"The less you know the better you sleep."*
>
> **Russian proverb**

Final roundup of questions

We are basically done now, apart from a short question in the next chapter which should bring you full circle back to the beginning. If that sounds retrogressive, don't worry. Questions in business, and in life generally, never end. They should be a source of fascination, not irritation. The day you stop questioning things, you might as well measure up for your coffin. So as a final roundup, let's look for the last time at the sequence we have been investigating throughout this book.

So what?
You should be able to answer this retort with a clear reason, such as "because it's thoroughly worthwhile and will benefit the business".

Why?

You should know precisely why you are doing something.

How?

You should have worked out precisely how it can be done, without fudging the answer.

Who?

You should have established exactly who will do it, and they must have agreed to do so. (As I warned in Chapter 7, double-check that you have not written "Action: Emma" on a document somewhere and failed to let her know – this does not count as deciding who will do something, because she probably won't.)

When?

You should have sorted out all the timings, and have had them all agreed to be acceptable by the people who have to deliver them.

Where?

You should have established in a crystal clear way where the work will be done, so that any vague elements of virtual working have been exposed and thrashed out.

Do we really need to do this?

You should have asked this question again towards the end, just to make absolutely sure that no fanciful thinking has crept into the mix.

Something must be wrong if...

You should have completed the rest of this sentence, if necessary several times over, just in case the open-ended nature of the other questions has allowed anyone not to articulate that there is actually a problem.

Are we there yet?

You should have posed this question regularly as the project progresses, in order to provide you with highly specific information about what stage you have reached at any given time.

What?

You will only need to use this question as a last-gasp measure – have a look at Chapter 10 to see why.

Ready to make the leap?

You may have been applying some of the stuff in this book as we have gone along, in which case, well done. If not, are you ready to make the leap? Go on, being inquisitive will revolutionize your life.

> *"I do not know which makes a man more conservative – to know nothing but the present, or nothing but the past."*
>
> **John Maynard Keynes**

Are we there yet? summary

1. We can learn a lot from children's lines of inquiry.
2. Surviving long journeys is a knack we need to acquire in life, and in business.
3. *Are we there yet?* can be used to pinpoint whether things are on course or not.
4. External *Are we there yet?* questions may reveal the truth, but not always.
5. Internal *Are we there yet?* questions will flush out what the external ones don't.

6. Problems are best dealt with when you depersonalize the issue.
7. Originality is a great asset to problem-solving, and you may wish to deploy the power of synectics in order to help.
8. Consider other childish questions.
9. Have a final roundup of questions, and then get on with it.
10. Are you ready to make the leap?

Exercise: Questioning everything like a child

1. If you have children of speaking age, spend some proper time with them and pay very close attention to their lines of inquiry. Don't patronize them with palliative answers. Write down what their questions are.

2. Now apply these questions to your business. You may be delighted to find that they contain no jargon whatsoever because, unlike grown-ups, children don't invent jargon to provide themselves with a linguistic cocoon.

3. If you have slightly older children, say 10–18 years old, ask them what questions mattered most to them when they were younger. Use their answers as stimulus to see if you can remember how you questioned the world when you were younger.

4. Sweep up all these ideas and use them as a platform to rediscover your sense of inquisitiveness. Apply this to your work by all means, but certainly apply it to your life.

What? Author's Postscript

A postscript more than a chapter. The What? *question and whether you really need to ask it. What's it all for? The meaning of life, and work. Do you really know what you are doing? If you can't answer the* What? *question, then go back to the beginning.*

The *What?* question

This final part of the book is not so much a chapter as a short comment on the *What?* question, and the circular nature of patterns of questions that take you back to where you started. I thought long and hard about whether to make the *What?* question an integral part of the question chain. Ultimately, I decided not. Don't get me wrong, *What?* is undoubtedly a brilliant question. I'm a great fan. It forces people to define or identify what they are talking about, and that's essential for any decent piece of communication.

However, after much consideration, I took the view that, if you haven't worked out *what* you are referring to, you really shouldn't be reading this book, or possibly embarking on anything at all, however simple. That is to say, if you haven't determined what you are talking about, then there is no point in asking any of the other questions. You would simply be trying to establish clarity around something that was fundamentally vague in the first place. It's what a colleague of mine used to call nailing a jelly to the wall.

"Stupidity has a knack of getting its way."

Albert Camus

What's it all for? The meaning of life, and work

I happen to write about business things, but if you have read even a fraction of this book, you will know that I regard business as being indivisible from life in general. It doesn't work if you are one person at work and another at home. You need to get the blend right, and introducing some of the more human qualities from your personal life into your business *modus operandi* is a thoroughly worthwhile exercise. Everybody needs to work to live, so you might as well make it as pleasurable as possible. In that sense then, the meaning of life and work becomes the same. Be inquisitive, be true to yourself, and enjoy it.

Say what?

So the *What?* question certainly has its purpose. If it becomes apparent that you do need to use it, then you must use it at the very beginning of any process, otherwise every other question will be pointless thereafter.

> *"The trouble with the world is that the stupid are cocksure and the intelligent are full of doubt."*
>
> **Bertrand Russell**

You should develop the general habit of defining what something is as a matter of course. In doing so you will eliminate all woolly subject matter that is too vague to be worth concentrating on, and at the same time use language that is clearer and more specific. This approach is not intended to turn you into a pedant – simply to make you better at explaining what you want, and to prevent you from falling prey to nebulous requests that beguile you into sounding as though they are well formulated.

What are you doing?

You should ask yourself *What am I doing?* many times a day. If you ever get that strange feeling that you are doing something and you don't know why, then stop immediately. Think. What is the point of this? If you can come up with a satisfactory explanation, then carry on. If you can't, do nothing else until you have been able to establish what you are doing. As is the case with most of the questions in this book, it sounds incredibly basic, but we all know millions of people do hundreds of tasks every day without really knowing why.

> *"Common sense is the collection of prejudices acquired by the age of eighteen."*
>
> **Albert Einstein**

If you don't know what you are doing...

If you don't know what you are doing, then why are you doing it? Your time and energy are too precious to waste in this way. By being more inquisitive, you can improve your happiness, and probably increase your life expectancy.

> *"He that overvalues himself will undervalue others, and he that undervalues others will oppress them."*
>
> **Samuel Johnson**

Back to the beginning

The series of questions in this book are circular. Start with *What?* if you really need to define clearly what you are talking about. But try to have that clear in your mind anyway, otherwise you may well not be ready to proceed at all. Move through the series methodically: *So what?, Why?, How?, Who?, When?, Where?, Do we really need to do this?, Something must be wrong if...*, *Are we there yet?* And then go back to the beginning. Once you get the hang of it, you can go through this process many times a day, thereby saving yourself hours of effort on things that don't matter and that won't get you anywhere.

Good luck. And remember, next time a colleague or boss wheels round to your desk with a triumphant announcement, just look at them calmly, smile, and say: *So what?*

> *"Knowledge is ultimately available to everyone. Only true intuition, jumping from knowledge to an idea, is yours and yours alone."*
>
> **Bill Bernbach**

Exercise: What the @!*k am I doing?!

1. You may well be fed up with exercises by now, and I am not suggesting that you have to do any of them. But if you like them, try this one.

2. Write *What the @!*k am I doing*?! at the top of a blank piece of paper. Now write down the left-hand side all the main parts of your life that matter to you.

3. Stare at it for a while, and gradually fill in your response to the question under each topic. The precise form of the words doesn't matter – you might write okay/not okay, tick/cross, give it a mark out of ten, or a short comment such as 'brilliant' or 'disastrous'.

4. Analyse your findings. How many good things are there? How many bad? Obviously, we are hoping for all or mostly good. If there are one or two bad things, identify what they are and what can usefully be done to improve them. If there are lots of them, you may need to make wholesale changes in your life.

5. Write down separately what your course of action is going to be to improve the areas that you found wanting.

6. If necessary, repeat the entire process for your business as a separate exercise.

APPENDICES

Appendix I: Book Summaries

BOOK: *Dangerous Company*
AUTHORS: James O'Shea & Charles Madigan

What the book says

- Extreme caution is needed when dealing with management consultants.
- There is a lot of information about the workings of Andersen, Boston Consulting Group, Bain, McKinsey, Gemini and their clients.
- You can find their products in here too – BCG's matrix (Growth; fast/slow – Cash; high/low – fill in stars/dogs/cash cows/question marks), the balanced scorecard, and Gemini's transformation or re-engineering concept.
- It warns against fuzzy concepts like "world class" which cannot be defined or measured, and creating a "consulting fantasyland" which sounds reassuring but doesn't actually get you anywhere.
- Just before he died, McKinsey confessed that making real decisions in business is a lot harder than getting paid to advise people what to do – sometimes it is fine to admit that you don't have all the answers.

What's good about it

- There are many parallels to be drawn between client/ agency relationships and those between companies and consultants. There is a checklist of how to deal with consultants, which could equally apply to clients dealing with agencies:
  - *Why are you doing this?*
  - *Do you need outsiders?*
  - *Who will work on the business?*
  - *What will it cost?*
  - *Never give up control.*
  - *Don't be unhappy even for a day.*
  - *Beware of glib talkers with books.*
  - *Value your own employees.*
  - *Measure the process.*
  - *If it's not broken, don't try to fix it.*
- Being aware of these theories will increase your strategic capability.
- Consultants are better than agencies at applying market learnings from one client to another, and at repackaging their skills many times over.

What you have to watch

- This is not a classic marketing textbook where you can grab a few diagrams and claim you have read it – you need to absorb it and use the examples.
- The parallels with agency faults could shoot you in the foot if mishandled.

BOOK: *Flicking Your Creative Switch*
AUTHOR: Wayne Lotherington

What the book says

- Everyone can be creative, regardless of whether they think they are.
- Creativity is variously described as "the spark that ignites new ideas", "the infinite capacity that resides within you", and "shaping the game you play, not playing the game you find".
- Good ideas arise when we take something we already know (light bulb no. 1) and consider it in relation to another thing we already know but which is unrelated (light bulb no. 2). Merging them creates light bulb number 3 – the new idea.

What's good about it

- It explains the origin of the phrase "thinking outside the box". The Gottschaldt figurine, or nine-dot game, requires you to join all the dots without taking your pen off the paper. You can't solve it if you view it as a box.
- ROI is used to stand for relevance, originality and impact. Your ideas won't work if they do not have all three.
- Barriers to creativity have been placed in our way since childhood: *don't be foolish, grow up, work before play, do as you're told, don't ask questions, obey the rules, be practical*, and so on.
- There are six techniques which you can use in any awayday to generate ideas:
  - **Random Word:** take a noun randomly from somewhere and apply it to the subject. You can also use pictures.

- **Eyes of Experts:** choose three respected experts from other fields and consider how they would deal with your issue. There is a variation called Industrial Roundabout where you view it through a different category.
- **What's Hot?:** use popular current things to appeal to your audience.
- **Curly Questions:** use analogies, speculation, role reversal and imagination to rephrase the issue at hand so that more original answers emerge.
- **Exaggeration and Depravation:** over-exaggerate the benefits of a product, or push to ludicrous extremes what happens if it isn't present.
- **Exquisite Corpse:** based on surrealist thinking, different people randomly select five words to create a sentence in the pattern adjective/noun/verb/adjective/noun. For example, *The peculiar bicycle swims a brilliant banana.* Each word is then scrutinized to review the problem.

What you have to watch

- You need to control the exercises so they don't seem trivial.
- You need an open-minded client.

BOOK: *Herd*
AUTHOR: **Mark Earls**

What the book says

- It is subtitled "How to change mass behaviour by harnessing our true nature".
- The main point is that, whilst everyone else is banging on about individual choice and one-to-one marketing, in fact everybody just copies, or is influenced by, other people.
- As such, most attempts by marketers to alter mass behaviour fail because they are based on a false premise.
- This is why most government initiatives struggle to create real change, why so much marketing money fails to drive sales, why M&A programmes actually *reduce* shareholder value, and most internal change projects don't deliver any lasting transformation.

What's good about it

- It explains the "why" of our struggles to influence mass behaviour.
- Most of us in the West have misunderstood the mechanics ("the how") of mass behaviour because we have misplaced notions of what it means to be human.
- There is a huge range of diverse anecdotes and evidence – from Peter Kay and urinal etiquette to international rugby and the rise of the Arctic Monkeys – to show that we are, at heart, a "we" species, but one suffering from the "illusion of I".

- It challenges most standard conceptions about marketing and forces the reader to rethink the whole thing.
- The seven principles of herd marketing are:
  1. Interaction (between people)
  2. Influence (of certain people)
  3. Us-Talk (the power of word of mouth)
  4. Just Believe (stand for something and stick to it)
  5. (Re-)Light the fire (overcoming cynicism by restating the original idea)
  6. Co-creativity (let others join in)
  7. Letting go (you never were in charge of your brand)

What you have to watch

Nothing.

BOOK:	*Liar's Paradise*
AUTHOR:	**Graham Edmonds**

What the book says

- 80% of companies think that they are fraud-free, but a recent survey actually revealed fraud in 45% of them.
- There are seven degrees of deceit:
  1. **White lie**: told to make someone feel better or to avoid embarrassment.
  2. **Fib**: relatively insignificant, such as excuses and exaggerations.
  3. **Blatant**: whoppers used when covering up mistakes or apportioning blame.
  4. **Bullshit**: a mixture of those above combined with spin and bluff to give the best impression.
  5. **Political**: similar to bullshit but with much bigger scale and profile.
  6. **Criminal**: illegal acts from fraud to murder, and their subsequent denial.
  7. **Ultimate**: so large that it must be true. As Joseph Goebbels said: "If you tell a lie big enough and keep repeating it, people will eventually come to believe it."

What's good about it

- It confirms what we all suspect – that the workplace constantly bombards us with lies, fakery and spin.
- Case histories of Enron, Boo.com, the European Union and others provide the proof on a grand scale.
- Deconstructions of other levels of lying help the reader to navigate their way through the day-to-day types. You can then decide how to react.

- It has tips on how to suck up to the boss, pass the buck and endure meetings.
- Everybody should read the chapter on Lies and Leadership.

"The truth is more important than the facts." Frank Lloyd Wright

"Those that think it is permissible to tell white lies soon grow colour blind." Austin O'Malley

"Honesty may be the best policy, but it's important to remember that apparently, by elimination, dishonesty is the second-best policy." George Carlin

What you have to watch

- The book essentially condemns most corporate cultures and so needs to be viewed lightly by those who have to work in them.
- There is a moral dilemma lurking within: do you tell the truth and get trod on, or join the liars?

BOOK: *Simply Brilliant*
AUTHOR: **Fergus O'Connell**

What the book says

- The best ideas aren't always complicated and the incredibly straightforward stuff is often overlooked in the search for a complex answer.
- Many smart people lack the set of essential skills which could roughly be described as "common sense".
- There are seven principles here that can be adapted for attacking most everyday problems:
  1. Many things are simple – *despite our tendency to complicate them.*
  2. You need to know what you're trying to do – *many don't.*
  3. There is always a sequence of events – *make the journey in your head.*
  4. Things don't get done if people don't do them – *strategic wafflers beware!*
  5. Things rarely turn out as expected – *so plan for the unexpected.*
  6. Things either are or they aren't – *don't fudge things.*
  7. Look at things from other's point of view – *it will help your expectations.*

What's good about it

- In a world of over-complication, asking some simple questions can really make your life easier. For example:
  - What would be the simplest thing to do here?
  - Describing an issue or a solution in less than 25 words.
  - Telling it as though you were telling a six-year-old.

- Asking whether there is a simpler way.
- Try writing the minutes of a meeting before the meeting – then you'll know what you want to get out of it.
- It highlights the difference between duration and effort. *"How long will it take you to have a look at that?" "About an hour."* But when?
- It explains the reasons why things don't get done: confusion, over-commitment, inability – usually busy people never say there's a problem!
- Plan your time assuming you will have interruptions – the *"hot date"* scenario.

What you have to watch

- The orientation is very much based on a project management perspective, which is fine if you are one, but others may prefer to cherry-pick the most applicable ideas.
- Anyone who flies by the seat of their pants would have to be very disciplined to apply these ideas. It's a bit like dieting.

BOOK: *S.U.M.O. (Shut Up, Move On)*
AUTHOR: **Paul McGee**

What the book says

- Everybody has the ability to grab their life by the scruff of the neck and make it work for them.
- When dealing with tricky issues, seven questions can help you to S.U.M.O.:
  1. Where is this issue on a scale of 1–10?
  2. How important will this be in six months' time?
  3. Is my response appropriate and effective?
  4. How can I influence or improve the situation?
  5. What can I learn from this?
  6. What will I do differently next time?
  7. What can I find that's positive in this situation?

What's good about it

- There are some thought-provoking concepts.
- *Change your T-Shirt* – this is the VICTIM T-shirt that stops people moving on.
- *Develop Fruity Thinking* – this is more productive than Faulty Thinking, which includes the Inner Critic, Broken Record, Martyr Syndrome and Trivial Pursuits (repetitive and petty criticism that gets you nowhere).
- *Hippo Time is OK* – a brief period of wallowing is acceptable as a bridge to move on, based on the understanding that sometimes you have to go down to go up.
- *Remember the Beachball* – if a huge multi-coloured beachball fills a room, people at one end will think it is red, white and blue; those at the other will see it as orange, green and yellow. Both are right, so bear in

mind other people's viewpoints when trying to impose yours.

- *Learn Latin* – Carpe Diem, seize the day and make the most of opportunities.
- *Ditch Doris Day* – reject the idea in her famous song, *Que Sera, Sera* (What will be, will be). You are not controlled by events, you control them.

What you have to watch

- If you are a fairly sorted person who is not riddled with self-doubt, there may be nothing in this book for you.
- Some of the ideas are so common-sensical that they border on the simplistic.
- The Fruity Thinking concept isn't really developed properly.

BOOK: *The Art Of Creative Thinking*
AUTHOR: John Adair

What the book says

- Once you understand the creative process, you can train yourself to listen, look and read with a creative attitude. Techniques include:
- Using the stepping stones of analogy (use normal things to suggest new uses).
- Make the strange familiar and the familiar strange (analyse what you don't know about something you know well).
- Widen your span of relevance (many inventions were conceived by those working in other fields).
- Be constantly curious.
- Practise serendipity (the more you think, the more it appears you are in "the right place at the right time").
- Making better use of your Depth Mind (trust your subconscious to sort things out and generate solutions once you have "briefed it").
- Learn to tolerate ambiguity.
- Suspend judgement.
- No one should wait for inspiration – you have to make it happen.

What's good about it

- This rather brilliant short book was originally written in 1990, so it is not riddled with modern jargon or method. It just tells it straight.
- Chance favours the prepared mind. By keeping your eyes open, listening for ideas and keeping a notebook, you can capture stimuli as they occur.

- It is full of inspirational comments from artists, scientists and philosophers.

"I invent nothing; I rediscover." Rodin

"Everything has been thought of before, but the problem is to think of it again." Goethe

"Discovery consists of seeing what everyone has seen and thinking what nobody has thought." Anon

What you have to watch

- Nothing. Everyone should read it for life use as well as just creative thinking in business.

BOOK: *The Cluetrain Manifest*
AUTHORS: **Levine, Locke, Searls & Weinberger**

What the book says

- The "cluetrain" is simply following a chain of conversations on the web.
- It is the end of business as usual because these conversations have changed for ever the way companies need to interact with their customers.
- In fact, markets (customers) are now usually more intelligent than companies because they can exchange information faster.
- Customers and employees are openly communicating so there are no secrets any more – one-way rhetoric from head office simply doesn't wash.
- Companies that choose to ignore this are missing a massive opportunity.
- There are 95 theses designed to ignite a debate.

What's good about it

- It is interesting to consider that the appeal of the Internet is not the technology but people's desire to tell stories and communicate generally.
- It must be true that an employee who tells the internal truth about a company can cause havoc, so companies need to know how to deal with it. There is an example of someone in Canada being overcharged for a car service – the chain ends when an employee of the dealership explains how they load prices.
- Communications never should be one-way, and this is a poignant reminder.

- The 95 theses can be read in 5 minutes and are a good source of controversial quotes.

What you have to watch

- It is a series of essays and as such lacks coherence.
- It is "magnificently overstated", according to one critic – "brilliant and impossible at the same time".
- Most companies won't enjoy hearing the contents so care is needed in how to raise this whole area with clients, and what can realistically be done.

BOOK: *The Long Tail*
AUTHOR: **Chris Anderson**

What the book says

- Endless choice is creating unlimited demand.
- Traditional business models suggest that high-selling hits are required for success. These are at the high-volume end of a conventional demand curve.
- But in the Internet era, the combined value of the millions of items that only sell in small quantities can equal or even exceed the best sellers.
- Modest sellers and niche products are now becoming an immensely powerful cumulative force. In this respect, many "mass" markets are turning into millions of aggregated niches.

What's good about it

- This is a very original and thought-provoking book. It takes a while to get into, but it's worth it.
- It introduces reasonably complicated mathematical theory in a user-friendly way, particularly micro-analysis of the very end of a very long tail. This is where helpful truths about the economics of your market can be seen properly.
- Contemporary examples from music (radio and album sales), books and films lend a populist slant to the theory, which should appeal widely.
- Old theories such as the 80/20 rule receive a thorough going-over. It's never exactly 80/20, and the percentages can apply to different things (products, sales or profits). And they don't add up to 100.

- The nine big rules of the *Long Tail* are:
  1. Move inventory way in… or way out.
  2. Let customers do the work.
  3. One distribution method doesn't fit all.
  4. One product doesn't fit all.
  5. One price doesn't fit all.
  6. Share information (lose control).
  7. Think "and", not "or".
  8. Trust the market to do your job.
  9. Understand the power of free.

What you have to watch

- The model works best with true Internet and digital products that do not take up any storage space. For example, Amazon books still require storage space that has a cost. I-tunes do not. So careful thought is required as to the nature of the market you are analysing.

BOOK: *The Tipping Point*
AUTHOR: **Malcolm Gladwell**

What the book says

- Little things can make a big difference.
- Explains and defines the "tipping point" – the moment at which ideas, trends and social behaviour cross a threshold, tip and spread like wildfire.
- Just as one sick person can start an epidemic, very minor adjustments to products or ideas can make them far more likely to be a success.
- The overall message of the book is that, contrary to the belief that big results require big efforts that are beyond the capacity of the single individual, one imaginative person applying a well-placed lever can move the world.

What's good about it

- It is optimistic in outlook and suggests that individuals can make a significant contribution. It cites the example of Paul Revere who, in 1775, overheard a conversation and rode all night to warn Americans in Boston that the British would attack in the morning. The Americans were ready and defeated them.
- The three areas (below) are a good working template for all communications:
  1. *The Law of the Few* – the idea that the nature of the messenger is critical.
  2. *The Stickiness Factor* – the quality of the message has to be good enough to be worth acting on.
  3. *The Power of Context* – people are exquisitely sensitive to changes of time, place and circumstance.

What you have to watch

- The three areas aren't that original – they are roughly similar to medium, message and target audience.
- It is easy to get distracted by the three groups of people who may start a tipping point: *Connectors* (people who know a lot of people), *Mavens* (those who accumulate knowledge, but are not persuaders), and *Salesmen* (people who are very persuasive). These may be more relevant to PR than paid-for communication.
- It is quite American, with many examples relating to the USA (for example, how removing graffiti reduced the crime rate in New York in the eighties). Thought is needed with regard to application elsewhere.
- Even if a marketing strategy overtly sets out to create a tipping point, they are so idiosyncratic and hard to predict that it might not work.

BOOK: *The World Is Flat*
AUTHOR: Thomas L. Friedman

What the book says

- Knowledge and resources are connecting all over the world, effectively flattening it.
- These forces, which include blogging, online encyclopaedias and podcasting, can be a force for good – for business, the environment and people everywhere.

There are ten forces that flattened the world:

1. 11/9/89: the day the Berlin Wall came down.
2. 8/9/95: the launch of the World Wide Web.
3. Work Flow Software: making much more stuff happen seamlessly.
4. Uploading: everybody can contribute to online communities.
5. Outsourcing: your company may not do much of what it sells to customers.
6. Offshoring: many US services are provided in India.
7. Supply-chaining: making sure everything arrives in the right place, fast.
8. Insourcing: for example, UPS repair all of Toshiba's laptops.
9. In-forming: Google, Yahoo! and MSN websearch inform people at the touch of a button.
10. The steroids: digital, mobile, personal, and virtual devices all fuel the machine.

He also outlines The Triple Convergence. This is where new players, a new playing field, and new processes all come together in "horizontal collaboration".

What's good about it

- It is a superb synthesis of all the developments you can think of in modern communications.
- Many of the elements of globalization are recorded in a fragmented way. Here they are all drawn together in one place.
- It is very thought-provoking because it highlights how recent so many of the developments we now take for granted are.
- There are lots of anecdotes and examples to bring the drier technological points to life.

What you have to watch

- It is very long, so you need a bit of stamina to get through it.

BOOK: *Welcome to the Creative Age*
AUTHOR: **Mark Earls**

What the book says

- Old-fashioned marketing is dead. It used to be about selling more than the other guy, but now it is mistakenly embraced as an organizational philosophy.
- Creativity is our greatest gift, but we don't always use it effectively.
- Four big things have changed the face of marketing:
  1. There is too much of everything (every market is over-supplied).
  2. The end of the consumer (people are confident and understand what marketing people are doing).
  3. The rise of the consumer as activist.
  4. The demanding employee (the company man is dead).

What's good about it

- *Creative Age Ideas*: assume that audiences are neither listening nor interested; don't try to fit in (in fact usually challenge); and are often the result of strongly held beliefs, not rational analysis.
- These are renamed *"Purpose Ideas"*: what counts is what you want to change about the world (what is your purpose?).
- The "added-value banana" anecdote, in which one is packaged as a "fresh banana snack" ideal to be eaten on the move (all of which we know already), is salutary about the insanity of much modern marketing.
- The book tells you how to have ideas like this by identifying your purpose (not your positioning) and deciding on interventions (it's what you *do* that counts).

- There are lots of good mantras such as "leave your agenda at the door", "the brand ties you to the past", "benchmarking yourself into a corner", and "control is an illusion we are better off without".
- There are whole chapters on why advertising people don't know how advertising works, and how to put *Purpose Ideas* at the heart of a business.

What you have to watch

- Depending on what you do for a living, some of this might be unsettling and make the opposite of the case you desire, for example *"Fact: most of the people in an ad agency are not paid to be inventive or creative but to manage and service the ad-factory machinery."*
- Any book that declares the death of something has to propose new ways forward. This one only half does, by setting you thinking for yourself.

Appendix II: Origin of Time Divisions

January: from the Latin *Januarius*, an adjective describing the month of Janus. He was the Roman god of doorways, passages, and bridges. In art he is depicted with two heads facing opposite ways. Janus-faced has also come to mean two-faced or hypocritical.

February: from the Latin *Februarius mensis*, meaning month of expiation, purification, or atonement.

March: from *Martius* (the month of Mars), the god of war and the father of Romulus and Remus, the brothers who were suckled by a she-wolf and later went on to establish Rome.

April: from the Etruscan *Aprilis*.

May: from *Maius*, relating to the Greek goddess Maia. She was one of the seven Pleiades placed as stars in the sky by her father Atlas, to save her from the pursuit of Orion.

June: from *Junius*, a long line of aristocratic Roman families.

July: named after Gaius Julius Caesar (100–44 B.C.), a Roman statesman.

August: from the Roman emperor Augustus (63 B.C.–14 A.D.). The name means dignified or imposing.

September: from *septem*, meaning seven.

October: from *octo*, meaning eight.

November: from *novem*, meaning nine.

December: from *decem*, meaning ten.

Monday: Old English (OE), day of the Moon.

Tuesday: OE, from the Germanic god Tiw, their equivalent of Mars.

Wednesday: OE, from the Germanic god Odin (Mercury).

Thursday: OE, day of thunder, named after Germanic thunder god Thor.

Friday: OE, from the Germanic goddess Frigga (Venus).

Saturday: OE, day of Saturn.

Sunday: OE, day of the Sun.

Year: from the Germanic *gear*, the time taken by the Earth to make a revolution round the Sun (365 days).

Month: from OE *monath*, relating to the Moon.

Week: OE, from the Germanic *wice*, probably meaning sequence or series.

Hour: from Anglo-Norman *ure*, meaning season.

Minute: from Latin *minuta*, made small.

Second: from Latin *secunda minuta*, the second operation of dividing an hour by 60.

Appendix III: Gottschaldt Figurine Solutions

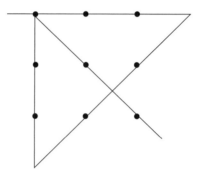

Fig. III.1:   Gottschaldt figurine solution No. 1

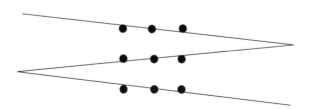

Fig. III.2:   Gottschaldt figurine solution No. 2

Appendix IV: Bibliography

Dangerous Company, James O'Shea and Charles Madigan (Nicholas Brealey, 1997)

Flicking Your Creative Switch, Wayne Lotherington (John Wiley & Sons, 2003)

Herd. How to change mass behaviour by harnessing our true nature, Mark Earls (John Wiley & Sons, 2007)

Liar's Paradise, Graham Edmonds (Southbank, 2006)

Simply Brilliant, Fergus O'Connell (Prentice Hall, 2001)

S.U.M.O., Paul McGee (Capstone, 2006)

Teach Yourself Growing Your Business, Kevin Duncan (Hodder & Stoughton, 2006)

Teach Yourself Running Your Own Business, Kevin Duncan (Hodder & Stoughton, 2005)

The Art Of Creative Thinking, John Adair (Kogan Page, 1990/2007)

The Cluetrain Manifesto (The end of business as usual), Rick Levine, Christopher Locke, Doc Searls, David Weinberger (Pearson, 2000)

The Long Tail, Chris Anderson (Random House, 2006)

The Tipping Point, Malcolm Gladwell (Little, Brown, 2000)

The World Is Flat, Thomas L. Friedman (Penguin, 2006)

Welcome to the Creative Age, Mark Earls (John Wiley & Sons, 2002)

INDEX